"A great book. Christine Mallouhi sees what only one born an outsider, but who through marriage has become an insider, can see, and she writes as only a hand can write that has been held by one born an insider and the One who became an insider for us all."

J. Dudley Woodberry, Professor of Islamic Studies and Dean Emeritus, School of World Mission, Fuller Theological Seminary

"Christine Mallouhi's *Miniskirts, Mothers and Muslims* comes out of 30 years of rich experience as a Western Christian woman living in the Arab world. She writes from as close to the inside of the culture as it is possible to get and is an honest guide in the nuances that will help others live respectfully. A 'must read' for those wishing to live in the Muslim world with integrity and honour. We heartily recommend it."

Tim and Merridie Costello, Urban Seed, Melbourne, Australia, and CEO World Vision, Australia

"I have never read a book quite like this one: full of insights into Arab culture and Muslim people, men as well as women. The author draws on her long and rich experience in the Arab world. She tells real-life stories which are worth volumes of academic research. This is a remarkable achievement for an outsider. True: she has the rare privilege of being the wife of a skilful Arab writer. The book will provide the reader with a wide open window from which to look at Arabs and Muslims as they really are, without the clichés of Western media."

Dr Chawkat Moucarry, Lecturer in Islamic Studies, All Nations Christian College

"Although I have lived for 36 years in Pakistan and travelled in many Muslim countries and areas, I am enriched, enlightened and refreshed by reading Christine Mallouhi's up-to-date book. The numerous fascinating stories drawn from her own and her friends' experiences among Arabs, together with her perceptive analyses of different cultures, make clear the infinite varieties of the Islamic world. I used the 1994 edition of Christine's book in my classroom and distance-learning teaching, as a basis for discussion in preparing Christians to cross cultures and live among Muslims. Much has happened to the world in the last ten years and I am so grateful for this revised and updated version of *Miniskirts, Mothers and Muslims*, and commend it to all, both men and women, with interests in cross-cultural communication."

Dr Vivienne Stacey

Miniskirts, Mothers & Muslims

A Christian woman in a Muslim land

CHRISTINE A. MALLOUHI

MONARCH
BOOKS

Oxford, UK & Grand Rapids, Michigan

First published in the UK by Spear Publications.
Revised edition published in 2004 by Monarch Books,
(a publishing imprint of Lion Hudson plc),
Mayfield House, 256 Banbury Road, Oxford OX2 7DH
Tel: +44 (0)1865 302750 Fax: +44 (0)1865 302757
Email: monarch@lionhudson.com
www.lionhudson.com

Published in conjunction with Firm Foundations Trust
14 Hurst Way, Sevenoaks, Kent TN13 1QN, UK

UK ISBN 1 85424 662 3
US ISBN 0 8254 6051 4

Distributed by:
UK: Marston Book Services Ltd, PO Box 269,
Abingdon, Oxon OX14 4YN;
USA: Kregel Publications, PO Box 2607
Grand Rapids, Michigan 49501.

British Library Cataloguing Data
A catalogue record for this book is available
from the British Library.

Cover photo: Chris Steele-Perkins/Magnum Photos

Book design and production for the publishers by
Bookprint Creative Services
P.O. Box 827, BN21 3YJ, England.
Printed in Great Britain.

A WORD OF THANKS:

Thank you, Mazhar, my loving partner in life, who has made as many radical changes as I have, to blend two cultures and two persons into Christ. Thank you to my Mum, Valerie (Hutchins) Baker (and Dad, with the cloud of witnesses). Your support and sacrifices, as parents and grandparents, allowed me to follow my calling with the freedom of blessing. Thanks to Dr Diana Colby, a social scientist with an interest in Islam, whose insights and encouragement helped rebirth this book.

In memory of one of the great cloud of witnesses, Louis Massignon, who discovered Christ through the hospitality of a Muslim home in Baghdad.

CONTENTS

FOREWORD

It was during a visit to Tunis as a guest of the Mallouhis that Christine asked me to write a short introduction to her book. At first I wondered: what do I have to do with miniskirts, mothers and Muslims? I was also afraid that the book might be one more apologetical writing aimed at vilifying Islam.

I read Christine's manuscript, re-read it and read it a third time. I felt I was reading one of the most profound books of spirituality. It is founded on strong theology and on a thorough understanding of the Bible, aiming first at the promotion of self-esteem, self-respect and decency.

I regret not having had this extremely important and enlightening text during the past forty years of my ministry among Muslim and Christian Arabs. This book would have spared me trouble with local village communities, because of mis-understandings and unintentional shocks and insults committed innocently by volunteers. Many volunteers as well would have been deeply enlightened and concretely helped to behave in a way that would have gained them a good reputation and helped them influence society for the better.

The question in this book is not whether to wear, or not to wear, a veil or miniskirt. It does not question the limitations of one's own freedom, so much as attitudes and outside appearances that constitute a breakdown of respect for the principles of modesty of the Arab people. Our society takes pride in being conservative, a society where the family and social structure are still the main wellsprings for our physical and spiritual health.

It is a sign of civilisation and of maturity to get to know your hosts, and to learn to respect them. This will assist the testimony of the entire church, and help us to pass the message to others, while respecting their traditions, civilisation, culture, and social codes.

We hear so much about preparing to go to war, to smash people, to suffocate nations, to eliminate groups, to flush out enemies. The culture of fear and death is gaining ground in the remotest places on our small planet. Therefore it is our greatest responsibility to promote a culture of trust and peace. Is that not the core of the message of the Risen Christ to his followers: "I give you my peace"? In practice this means to do to others what you would wish them to do to you. Do not judge your neighbour – it is for the Lord to judge. Jesus urges, "Follow me. Walk with God. Practice justice and speak truth."

Remember that we are commissioned to preach God's compassion and love, but not to preach any specific civilisation, nationalism or private emancipation.

Christine Mallouhi proves through her book that she has a very deep and thorough experience and knowledge of Islamic and Arab society and mentality. She also has a genuine, pertinent and thought-provoking understanding of the pedagogy of the Man from Galilee, the Lord Jesus Christ, who respects every human being for sticking to his or her own environment, tradition, culture and civilisation and invites everyone to adhere to his calling to become a beloved child of God.

I commend this book with all the power of my heart. This is not a choice among other books to read. This is a must because it is an eye-opener to the hidden values of each civilisation.

Abuna Elias Chacour, Ph.D.
Bishop-elect of Jerusalem, Melkite church
Author of *Blood Brothers* and founder of Mar Elias Educational Institutions in Galilee

INTRODUCTION

Many readers skip the author's notes and dive into the first chapter. But you need these notes to unravel the book. You can still skip them, but I think you will end up returning to this beginning in order to understand the background to the stories.

This book is for Christians who are venturing among Muslims – for secular employment, humanitarian work, missionary work, or crossing the road to meet their neighbour – and who are concerned to have a testimony for Christ recognisable in Muslim culture. It is for Christians concerned to share faith and not sure what is going on between the lines. It makes the assumption that Christians will want to live honourably among Muslims for Christ's sake, and explores what that means.

The stories are from the cultures that Muslims living in the West either came from, or still observe, inside their homes in Western streets. They reveal the shadow side of Muslim culture that is invisible to most Westerners. I am writing as the Western wife of an Arab from a conservative Muslim family. This means that the stories emphasise women, but I hope that half of my readers are men, and have included stories for them too.

The term "Arab" is used to mean all the nationalities represented by the Arab League. My experience has been among Arabic-speakers, but Arabs are a minority among Muslims in the world. There are specific Islamic understandings that are common to all Muslims, but these will be applied differently in various societies and cultures. How to talk about Muslims in a general way is a problem which seems to have no suitable solution. For the sake of readability I have needed to lump people into general geographical areas, while recognising that there are differences between countries in those areas, and between towns and villages in the same country, and in class and education, and religious aspirations and devotion, and politics, which all make differences in how people live out their religion. Edward Said's famous quote about not lumping millions of Muslims into one sentence is still true, except that the numbers are growing. The term "Eastern" applies to the cultures stretching from Morocco through the Balkans to Manila, where the local custom may be common to both Christians and Muslims.

This book brings the experiences of Western Christians living in Muslim societies back home for other Christians to learn from. The stories are mainly from my own experiences in Morocco, Tunisia, Egypt, Jordan, Palestine, Lebanon, Syria, Turkey, the United Arab Emirates, Kuwait, Bahrain, Oman, Yemen and Malaysia, with additions from other contributors and areas.

The book is about people tending to be from a monocultural background, that of Western evangelical Christianity, going to people who also tend to be monocultural. I am writing for Westerners entering the world of those Muslims who tend to interpret the Quran as affirming women's subjugation to men, and who believe that strict propriety is to be evidenced in public behaviour and that covering the body is more spiritual than not covering it.

I usually picture the more conservative understanding of Islamic customs, preferring to err on the side of being too conservative rather than being too lax. I believe this is a biblical concept. It is easier to take a more conservative attitude on the behaviour spectrum and keep a good reputation, than to start at the other end of the spectrum.

The book is a personal chat with Western Christians. I mean by "Christians" those who have made a decision to follow Christ, rather than those simply born into a Christian society and inherited faith; those who affirm a high view of Scripture and allow this to dictate how they live. If it is not written for you, please remember the audience.

This book is attempting to describe aspects of two broad cultures that are both experiencing change. Both Muslims and Christians are making changes in their understanding of gender relations. Both religions have a whole range of interpretations over how their scriptures direct relations with the opposite sex. Experts like Clifford Geertz begin this discussion with disclaimers such as, "It is not only very difficult to discover the ways in which the shapes of religious experience are changing, or if they are changing at all, it is not even clear what sorts of things one ought to look at to find out."[1] English and Arabic share hundreds of similar proverbs, reminding us that the human experience is essentially the same. But what makes other cultures interesting to me are not the similarities, but the differences. People travel around the world at great expense and effort in order to experience a different style of life. If we were not interested in the differences, we would just sit at home, or travel only to the usual spots. I have tried to notice the unusual, and to ask myself why it is not the usual way I as a Westerner would act or think, and have then asked the people I live among what they understand about their actions.

I have chosen the stories, examples, and proverbs that show our differences, not to compare one with the other in order to prove that Christians are better than Muslims, or vice versa, but to highlight the areas where we have two options: we can either celebrate or be frustrated.

This book was first written about ten years ago. After I researched Western Christians living in Muslim countries, I found the same subjects were still relevant and needed. I have added new stories and new slants on the older stories, reflecting changes in Muslim societies and changes in my understanding of my own faith.

Be careful about the assumptions you bring to this book. In the last edition, I mentioned the wonderful times of fellowship we had had over a barbecue. Subsequently, American friends shipped a supermodel giant barbecue to north Africa. I was astounded when they told me it was because of what I wrote. At the picnic I had written about, we just piled up large stones lying on the ground.

Notes

1. Clifford Geertz, *Islam Observed: Religious Development in Morocco and Indonesia*, University of Chicago Press, 1968, p. 1.

CHAPTER ONE

LIVING BETWEEN THE LINES

The street in Tunis was crowded and the group around us grew, as newcomers joined each side of the argument. I had caused the fight and we were still in the middle, with some defending us and others against us. When two men began throwing punches and people scuttled for safety, or dive-bombed on top to add their weight to their view, one of the men flashed a card pronouncing himself "security police" and attempted to arrest us.

We had been sitting in a sidewalk coffee shop and I was watching a shoeshine man. He was sitting on a small stool, busily shining the shoes of a customer who was drinking coffee. His tools of trade were neatly packed in an unusual box and revealed a meticulous personality and pride in his work.

This Tunisian scene differed from shoeshine scenes in the West and therefore was very interesting. I took a photo. I should have asked the man for his permission first. One of his customers took offence and complained, "Why are you taking pictures of these common, low-class people? Look at all the big modern buildings around. Why don't you take pictures of those, instead of these sorts of scenes?" There was nothing interesting or different in large modern buildings and I did not consider them worth the film. This man's picture was valuable to me. It was something different, and he was an old artisan whose lifestyle could disappear as life changes and becomes more mechanised. The incident turned into the street fight. Bystanders and café customers got involved, with some defending our right to take whatever photos we liked, and others agreeing with the man. The incident was very upsetting and I was physically shaking.

What surprised me was that the shoeshine man did not object to the customer demeaning his status. I don't know if any of the people defending us were fighting for this issue. Traditionally, in Arab society, only certain work is honourable, such as the prestigious vocations of law and medicine. Blue-collar trades are not included. My father was a tradesman and he raised us to believe that all work is honourable and that the poor have dignity and status equal to the rich. In addition, I am influenced by my Australian culture that takes pride in siding with the underdog and the loser, and is suspicious of very competitive people and those who appear proud of class and wealth.

Life seems to "come alive" when you live in a culture other than the one you grew up in. This can be exciting, frightening, saddening, depressing, refreshing. To some it can be unbearable. It will certainly be mysterious. What is going on and why? The problem comes when we think we know the script. We can watch the movie and interpret all the action, believing we have it right. But at the end, we discover that we missed the clues and drew wrong conclusions about the important things. There was another between-the-lines movie playing out right before our eyes, but we didn't see it.

Rosemary finished washing the tiny demitasse coffee cups and hung them in the wooden dish stack that served as a cupboard. A small café situated on the sidewalk beneath her third floor apartment was frequented by male clientele day and night. The pungent odour of the tobacco in the men's water-pipes below wafted through the open windows, along with the afternoon call to prayer and the inevitable dust. She and her husband had moved to this city 18 months ago and were pleased with their progress. Tom was happy in his work, and some of his local colleagues had reached out to the couple to help them adjust to their new life. They were accepted amongst the neighbours, enjoyed many friendships, and were learning new ways of living and thinking. Daily life was a challenging adventure and they did not regret their decision to take up employment in this predominantly Muslim country.

There had been many opportunities to discuss deeper issues as their language ability improved and they were eagerly working towards that day when they could discuss their Christian faith with their friends in a culturally sensitive and meaningful way. They had already learnt much about Islam from their friends and were impressed by the Muslims' deep respect for God and the Holy Scriptures. Their neighbours taught them not to treat the Bible with contempt by placing it carelessly on the floor. They had even bought them a special bookstand of intricately carved wood in which to keep the Bible when it was not being read. The husband instructed them to place this on a high mantle or shelf in their home to demonstrate that they honoured God's Word. The faces of Rosemary's new Muslim friends filed through her mind, giving her a sense of peace in being accepted and joy in being able to share Christ's love with them. Her adjustment was much easier than she had expected. She was fitting in easily and was pleased with herself.

The doorbell broke in on her reverie. Opening the door, she found Mustafa, a young student whom Tom had met recently, who wanted to practise his English. He greeted her and asked for Tom. With a big, friendly smile she told him that Tom wasn't home and she was alone, but he could come in and wait for him. Following the rules she had learned about hospitality, she brought Mustafa refreshments while cheerfully chatting with him. She suggested, "Tom won't be long. Just make yourself at home while I finish some chores." So, while she worked around the house, he followed her as they conversed. He followed her to the kitchen, then to the sitting room and then back to the kitchen. Rosemary began to feel a little uneasy. Wherever she turned, there he was with a big smile! But her uneasiness turned to real surprise when Mustafa followed her into the bedroom, lit a cigarette and, taking it from his mouth, offered it to her. She didn't need to understand all of the vocabulary to know his intentions. Anger came to her rescue and with a burst of strength and a torrent of words she propelled him towards the front door. Looking perplexed, he gave up easily. But unbelievably, as he left, he shot back angry words blaming her! She noticed her next-door neighbour watching the scene with shock written all over her face. Rosemary closed the door and, sinking into the nearest chair, burst into tears. She didn't understand how things had gone so terribly wrong. How could Tom's friend think she had loose morals? Did others think the same?

This incident is not the beginning of a novel, but a real-life story of a friend of mine. It portrays just one area of the many misunderstandings and perplexities Christians face as they attempt to live out and share their faith across cultures.

Westerners are not raised to know all the local social nuances and may miss what is going on. We fail to grasp the motives behind words and actions and tend to concentrate on the verbal communication. Locals are usually reading between the lines: interpreting the non-verbal communication. Often what is not verbally communicated is just as important as the verbal communication. Rosemary did not have a clue that she was giving "come-on" signals to the young student. One of the things she did not understand was the concept of gender boundaries. Muslim women have a natural understanding of these boundaries, inculcated from childhood. It is not so much a list of "don'ts", but a sense of what is proper and what is not, concerning distance between the sexes. Outsiders to the culture have to learn these things. Like Rosemary, readers are probably surprised by this story and do not expect to find loose sexual behaviour in Muslim societies, because of the veils and their understanding that it is a strict society. Like Western societies, Muslim societies have double standards, but Muslims take these further than Western society, because women are expected to remain chaste, while this same standard does not apply with the same strictness to men. Mustafa's conduct was extreme, but it does illustrate a particular problem Western Christians will face.

Key values

Immoral, insensitive, irreverent, selfish and dirty – these are just some of the ways Christians have been perceived by Muslims. And I have to add from my own story above – troublemakers! What has gone wrong, so drastically closing the doors on our testimony? Much of the failure of Westerners to grasp the underlying premises of Muslim culture results from our failure to understand and appreciate Muslim self-perception.

There are foundational Islamic principles pervading the

Muslim world. Although there are many variations in the practices of the Islamic faith within the Muslim world, and also within the Arabic-speaking countries, we will find these same foundational principles in each culture.

The central premise is one of right conduct. This is the foundational characteristic and the practical expression of the community (*umma*) of Islam. In the Quran we read, "Ye are the best of peoples evolved for mankind. Enjoining what is right, forbidding what is wrong, and believing in God." Another translation says, "You are the best community that hath been raised up for mankind. Ye enjoin right conduct and forbid indecency; and ye believe in Allah" (Quran 3:110).

The Arabic word *munkar*, translated "wrong" and "indecency" in the above quotations, has many shades of meaning. It also means "not recognised", "disowned", "shocking", "detestable", and "abominable". In view of this, good or decent conduct must be recognisable to the Muslim as he or she understands it. In order for Muslims to perceive us as people of faith and principle, we need to express our spiritual values in ways that they can recognise, or we may be perceived as people without faith, or even as indecent. Notice that the word *munkar* carries the meaning "unrecognised", which equates to "shocking" or "indecent".

Muslims have fairly rigid ideas of what is correct and incorrect behaviour for people of faith. This belief in God and the excellence of his community is expressed by their correct behaviour and decency. "Right conduct" is the hallmark of the Muslim and covers every area of life, from within the family circle to duties in society. The Muslim is given specific regulations for displaying his faith in right conduct, from the intimacy of the marriage bed to governing a state. These regulations cover faith, morals and personal cleanliness.

Muslims receive wrong impressions of Christians, because Western Christians fail to appreciate important aspects of Muslim culture, particularly at points where proper conduct is very important. These values, such as decency, hospitality and community responsibility, are outworkings of the values of honour and shame. If we neglect or disdain these external expressions of faith in our life, we demonstrate that we have not attained to the excellence of the Muslim family. We fall short and therefore appear to have nothing worth offering to them.

Honour and shame

In both the above stories the underlying issue is honour and shame. The café customer was angry that I shamed his country's image by the subjects I chose for photos. Western culture is not an honour/shame culture. The simplest way to figure out if we come from one of these cultures is to look at how we go about furnishing our home. When we decorate our living room, we may place a chair in the best vantage spot to see the television. We may move it around the room, checking if it fits better in other places. Our choice is usually based on pragmatism or beauty. We do not feel that we must only put the chair in the honourable place for it. Do we know when it is in a dishonourable place? If you have no idea what I am talking about and want to build deep friendships with Muslims, then you could get off to a bad start. I assume that you do not want to unintentionally insult Muslims or their religion.

I once put the Quran-stand on the floor in a corner, thinking it might be OK on the floor if there were no holy book in it. My husband came home and, sure enough, it jumped jarringly into his vision. It needed to be moved to an honourable place, even without a book in it, because it was a stand for a holy book and could not be treated with contempt. We value holy books and could not treat the stand as if it were simply an artefact. It should be raised onto a table, then moved into a different corner, so that it wasn't near a door, but was deeper in the room. This meant moving a lounge chair into an inconvenient place, buying a table and an extension cord for the light next to the chair, and having the bookstand in an odd place that didn't go with the furniture and didn't look right. My impulse – to creatively decorate an empty corner – became quite complicated. So the stand went back to its original honourable place.

One of the Afghani prisoners released from the US prison at Guantanamo Bay claimed that one of the worst ways they were ill-treated was when guards flushed the Quran down a toilet. Muslims will not even put Scripture verses in the bathroom or toilet. A Western man greeted a Muslim in the public toilet in an airport, saying *"assalaam alaikum"* (God's peace be with you). The Muslim recognised his good intention and kindly, but firmly, explained that he should not bring God into the bathroom. It is not an honourable place to discuss God. Muslims often tell me that the West has "no sense of shame".

Prestige and appearances

In my experience, Muslim societies tend to emphasise "ascribed status", compared to the West which emphasises "achieved status".[1] Ascribed status societies confer prestige at birth, in the same way that Queen Elizabeth gained status by being born. A person's family background carries more weight than accomplishments, but accomplishments can help to acquire additional status. In achieved status societies, as in the West, prestige is gained by accomplishments, and takes time to build up. All societies have both forms of status, but a particular society will lean towards one or the other. In ascribed status societies people prefer to associate only with their equals, and attention focuses on those with high social status. This class rigidity means that the poor and uneducated tend to be looked down on, which is what happened in my story about the shoe-shine man.

Muslims tend to belong to societies where appearances (houses, clothing, the way hospitality is given) reflect on their identity. Westerners do not always attach the same importance to these things. A number of Arab women who visited Western countries commented to me that they were shocked because "Western women do not look after themselves. They don't care about their appearance." The gap can be even wider for Western Christians, whose interpretation of Scripture tends to down-play the importance of visual appearances.

"Ascribed status" thinking is usually recognised as a charac-teristic of segmental thinking, in which specific criteria are used to judge behaviour. Lingenfelter and Mayers describe segmen-tal thinking as follows:

> Dichotomy is that pattern of segmental thinking that exhibits great concern about the particulars of any problem or situation, with a tendency to reduce each to right and wrong options. . . . Dichotomistic thinking tends to categorize people into specific roles. Once a person is labelled, the label defines one's character and place, even though it may not be a valid assessment of the person.[2]

> Differences in thought patterns [between holistic and dichotomistic] produce significantly different, and often opposing, value orienta-tions. Segmental thinkers demand clear cut, black-and-white issues, insist on universal application of principle, and cannot feel secure unless their perceptions are recognized as correct. Holistic thinkers on the other hand, see most issues as gray (open for debate) rather than black and white. . . . A [person] entering another culture must realize that people evaluate others in very different ways . . .[3]

As an example of segmental and dichotomistic thinking, a young Arab woman once told me that she had stopped veiling, because she could not "do everything else required with it". She explained, "I was studying and could not easily pray five times a day. I could not do everything required, so I cannot do anything."

Social stratification

Such characteristics in society have implications for outsiders on the social scale. The class distinctions are integral to the development of circles of friends. Because of these distinctions it is difficult to try and mix classes. Historically, missionaries in the Muslim world worked with the lower classes, almost to the exclusion of the higher classes. I am not suggesting that Western Christians should only make friends among the higher classes. I believe the key issue is that whatever class we live among, high or low, we should choose a level within it that will give us a position of respect. Then people will deem us worthy enough for our words to be esteemed. The Syrian proverb "Whoever marries my mother will be my uncle" means: I will respect anyone who has higher status, or is more powerful than me. It does not matter who the person is. The issue again relates to honour. If we do not know how to live in a worthy manner, our words will not be esteemed.

Yet the way to be seen as an honourable person may seem strange to Westerners. It is not something we achieve by our own efforts. We need the group's stamp of approval. One way this is gained is through our friends. Often, knowing a highly esteemed person is the key to acceptance. Outsiders need friends among the prestigious people in their social milieu. The Arab proverb states, "Show me your friends and I will tell you who you are." If we are friends of "So-and-so" then we are people worth knowing. It doesn't matter if this person is a member of parliament or the head garbage collector. If the person is esteemed by the group, seek his or her friendship. This concept may sound unscriptural, but I believe that a study of the Scriptures reveals that Christ gives us this pattern to follow. The Lord Jesus understood the Eastern culture he lived in and told his disciples, "Whatever town or village you enter, search for some worthy person there and stay at his house until you leave."[4]

Seeking out these people is not in order to exploit them to reach your goals, no matter how valuable your project will be to the country. It is to allow the person to teach you how to live as an honourable person in their society. At the same time, this person takes you under their umbrella, giving you legitimacy by being your sponsor. A Western couple living in Syria said: "In both cities where we lived we had the unofficial sponsorship of the mayor without being socially at his level."

One of the missionaries from a desert hospital told me this story. When a sheikhdom invited the mission hospital to open its doors to the population during the last century, the sheikh himself was the sponsor, thus giving it legitimacy in the eyes of the desert people who had never seen foreigners in their land before. The sheikh took an active interest in how things worked out and personally taught the staff how to offer their services in an appropriate way to the community. He told them how to live honourably among the people, and his approval gave them legitimacy.

However, the basis for not living across diverse classes in Muslim culture is simply pragmatic. The culture will not allow you to do it. In class-rigid societies people try not to associate with those they perceive as below their social class.

In Cairo, many upper-class women I knew would not use public transport. The metro is very efficient and faster than driving a car into town, but they drove themselves by car or had a chauffeur drive them about. They refused to be forced into the classless equality necessary when sharing a train.

In Tunisia, during an afternoon tea party, one upper-class woman stated, "Nobody eats with their hands in this country any more." Another observed, "Sexual segregation has died out and it is normal for couples to date." These statements may have been true within their class, although the latter statement was violently opposed by other women who declared they would never allow their daughters to date. But both statements are not representative of the country as a whole. We had friends in country areas where we ate with our hands, and on occasions went with upper-class friends back to the country areas where they came from, when they also ate with their hands. Segregation is still practised in parts of the country. These women were out of contact with the majority of their fellow countrywomen because they did not mix with others out of their class. They successfully managed not to mix beneath their class and did not know how the majority in their country lived. An interesting book displaying this attitude is *Out of Iran* by Sousan Azadi. An Iranian woman from high society, the author found herself in constant difficulties with her religious in-laws from a lower class. She lived a liberal Westernised lifestyle in Iran and was out of touch with the beliefs and practices of the majority of Iranians. For example, she didn't know it was not acceptable to wear perfume at her husband's funeral. Perfume is for celebrations, not funerals. The classes will not mix with each other, so it is difficult, and idealistic, to attempt to live among both high and low classes at the same time.

Certain behaviour is expected of those who hold a particular status. For example, teachers' friends are usually colleagues. A local teacher would not have many close friends amongst day labourers. A Western Christian in central Asia writes:

> I have noticed the class distinctions among my friends. I have very poor friends here in my neighbourhood, and wealthy ones I met through my husband's job. When they drop by my house, they sit together and talk. We laugh and enjoy ourselves. It is as though we are all equal. This does not carry over once they leave the house. One day, one of my poor friends said she had seen one of my rich friends at the bazaar. I asked how she was doing, and was told that they had not actually talked to each other. They had only nodded in passing.

Were they just too busy to stop and talk? More likely, it was because they avoided each other because of their class distinctions.

When expatriates ignore the class hierarchy, it can give rise to suspicions. Locals often attribute base ulterior motives for making friends across classes. Many of the Muslim countries in which Christians live today were until recently dominated by colonial powers, mainly Western. This is still remembered as a painful experience, and influences the way people think about us. Innocent aid workers and missionaries are sometimes confused with espionage agents. Spies are known to gather information from varied sources by moving across all classes, asking lots of questions and trying to learn the local language well. Newcomers intending to live in the local country also do these things. Muslim authorities today still cannot understand why an educated or wealthy foreigner would want a friendship with someone beneath their perceived class, unless they had an ulterior motive. When missionaries make local friends from lower social circles than where they live, the authorities may well accuse them of preying on the poor and weak by enticing them to become Christians.

In one town, the authorities accused a Western university professor of missionary activities because biblical texts turned up in his English literature course, and he had friends amongst his students. We knew him well and knew he had no faith in any god at all. One of the other points against him was that he was a family man with young children. The town consensus was that foreign family men were probably missionaries, single men were probably gay, and everyone else was probably a spy. There was no category, therefore, for most of the foreigners in the town.

Missions giving humanitarian aid are often accused of trying to buy faith with enticements. An Egyptian magazine described missionary activity as follows:

> [It] involved giving medicine and wealth and books to the poor of the region and then entering from this door into the minds and hearts of those in need, opening discussion which ended with people leaving their religion, stirring up feelings, and igniting sectarian strife by foreign hands . . .[5]

Some locals are so suspicious that even the International Red Cross has been accused of this. Many Western Christians move into local communities without a clue that these types of suspicions hang over them.

Just expressing personal faith can generate many problems. Once, when the police were questioning my husband about why he was sharing his faith, he was asked to name those with whom he had spoken about Christ. Since he has a personal commitment to mention Christ to every person with whom he has a meaningful conversation, he could readily name most people in town. He deliberately chose to name the leading men in that society, beginning with the chief of police. The police officer quickly interrupted saying, "Oh, that's fine. We don't have to worry about those men. They are educated and powerful enough to know where they stand. You can talk to those people. It is the poor and needy or otherwise underprivileged people we need to protect from exploitation." My husband did not distribute Christian literature, nor preach, nor try to proselytise. He discussed faith with friends wanting to have a faith discussion. One wonders, is free enquiry and thinking exploitation?

Christ and social class

How did Christ deal with the stratified class society he lived in? He both challenged it and worked within its limitations. Christ treated every person with respect and deliberately went out to the marginalised. He attended their parties in their homes. He allowed the repentant outcast woman to interrupt Simon's dinner and wipe his feet with her tears. But Christ worked within the confines of the society of his day and he did not insist that the woman join Simon's upper-class dinner party. He did not forcibly turn the institutions of society upside down in his lifetime. He confronted their prejudices through surprising actions to individuals. Jesus demonstrated that even in oppressive limitations, the poor could be set free from all that enslaves the spirit. He challenged everyone and restored their self-respect.[6] The seeds he left, in deeds and teaching, flowered over the centuries into great social reforms as his followers took them up at the appropriate times. As we help individuals to experience new life in Christ, this inner change results in new attitudes and behaviour. We expect these people will challenge harmful behaviours in their societies: in both East and West.

At times Christ utilised local customs. When he was about to enter a town he sent his disciples ahead to announce his coming and get a room ready, as if he were royalty. At other times he challenged them. He accompanied a man of high status on a life-and-death emergency for his daughter, but he let the man wait while he stopped to talk with an outcast woman who had been bleeding for twelve years. What kind of person would insult a ruler by stopping to give attention to an outcast woman at the bottom of the social scale in a life-and-death emergency? He allowed the ruler's daughter to die (temporarily), in order to heal a long-term illness that could have waited a few hours until after the home visit.[7] We are reminded again of Gandhi and Wilberforce and others who challenged their societies head on, and changed them, because they were insiders with influence. Few outsiders to Muslim culture will have the status and acceptance to implement significant social change. They are more likely to be seen as prejudiced Western Christian imperialists.

How many things can Western Christians actively support or challenge in Muslim society? This demands a personal and individual response. I decided I could only successfully drive in one lane at a time and not criss-cross the other lanes of class distinctions, women's rights, female circumcision, religious, political and intellectual freedom, and equal opportunities for education. I needed to direct energy to the main things I feel called by God to do, and leave the other issues for those able to make a difference. My sense of God's purpose for me in the Muslim world is to live *among* locals, in the deepest understanding of becoming one (as much as is possible for a foreigner), and to live for Christ. I do not accept class distinctions, nor gender discrimination, but I don't think that I can personally make any significant difference to these issues on a societal level. I treat the person in front of me in a way that reflects my convictions and faith, and I leave the changes in society to those Muslims who have inside influence and convictions to change these things. I also feel called to stand with the Palestinian people in their struggle for justice. To help Muslims see Christ in a new way and to bring justice to the Palestinians is enough for one life! The Arabic proverb "You cannot carry two watermelons in one hand" sums up my approach.

We currently live in Lebanon among the upper middle classes. We also have good friends among the poor and from the refugee camps. They visit in our home and we visit in theirs, but I cannot force my neighbours and these other friends to regularly mix together. It is not just the rich who are uncomfortable; neither group is comfortable and meeting together occasionally is all they will accept. There is also some discomfort between secular Muslims and Islamists when socialising together: they have little in common. In fact, they often choose not to socialise together and will only meet in the coincidental moments of daily life. Some very conservative Muslims will not attend family weddings if there will be both men and women present and dancing. We can move between these groups and enjoy them all, but these groups usually have more fun when they are not mixed.

During a get-together of neighbours, one of the women mentioned that she had come home in a taxi. She reported that when the driver arrived at their building, he had told her that he was related to one of the families who lived there and he had given the family name of one of the other women present at the get-together. The woman named looked offended and said, "We do not have a taxi driver in our family and I don't know any of those kinds of people. Anyone could come up with our name. It's a well-known name." The women's tea gatherings are a cross-pollination of religious groups. However, these women are more comfortable with each other than they are with co-religionists from the refugee camps, because they are all from the same building. They are the same class.

Notes

1. John Macionis, *Society: The Basics*, Prentice Hall, New Jersey, 1995–2001, Chapter 4.
2. Sherwood G. Lingenfelter and Marvin K. Mayers, *Ministering Cross-Culturally: An Incarnational Model for Personal Relationships*, Baker Book House, Michigan, 2000, p. 5.
3. *ibid.*, p. 65.
4. Matthew 10:11.
5. *Ruz al Yousef*, Egypt, 28 December 1992.
6. Ray Simpson, *Exploring Celtic Spirituality: Historic Roots for our Future*, Hodder & Stoughton, London, 1995, p. 146.
7. Mark 5:21–43.

CHAPTER TWO

LIVING WITH STATUS

A good public image is very important in Muslim culture. In a Muslim home, compare the reception room to the private rooms that are not visible to guests. The show rooms will be beautifully decorated, with the emphasis on impression rather than comfort, whereas the kitchen and family areas in comparison may be in a sad state of repair. In Istanbul, everyone who can afford it seems to have uncomfortable but stately-looking imitation Louis XVI furniture. The ornate living room furnished in this way is rarely used except for non-family guests. Families relax in more comfortably furnished, smaller rooms. The same is true of Morocco and other countries. In an Egyptian village, we once sat in the reception room of a mud house, on the same gaudy Louis XVI-style furniture (with red brocade and gold-painted wooden frame). A large glass chandelier hung close to our heads from the low ceiling, while chickens ran around our feet on the dirt floor.

Jordanian Christian friends with limited resources had no plumbing in their home. They claimed they couldn't afford to put it in. But they bought an expensive car that sat idle in the street outside their house. Once in a while, a relative took them for an outing, because no one in the house had a driver's licence. The desire for a good public image outweighed the daily inconvenience of having no plumbing. When their daughter got engaged and the groom's family paid a handsome bridewealth, she used the money for a fancy bedroom suite rather than unseen plumbing. She recognised that this decision would cost her many hours of hard labour, heating water in cans to wash children and clothes. The main bedroom already had a comfortable double bed, but image was more important.

Muslims recognise outward appearances as a way of making a statement of faith. Western Christians have a double-barrelled cultural and Christian value of believing that appearances are not important. We believe that "you can't tell a book by its cover". Appearances are not supposed to sway our judgements. Everyone should be given the chance to prove himself. Whereas the Arab proverbs "You know the book by its title" and "As much clothing you dress in, so much are you worth" vividly confront us with different ways of thinking. One Kurdish girl exclaimed to a Western woman who was having trouble understanding this, "Appearance is everything." People with limited resources will buy one chic outfit and wear it every day rather than appear outdated by wearing unfashionable clothes.

Sometimes Western Christians make non-verbal statements against Western affluence that are received differently in the Muslim world. We moved into a middle-class area in Cairo, furnished our first home too simply, and attempted to live across classes. Actually, we rented a furnished flat which was in very poor condition. There was little we could do to make it look more presentable on a tight budget. Upper-class people who met us outside our home were very warm until they visited us. Then, surprised at how we were living, they encouraged us to move to a better place. When this did not happen they dropped out of our lives. They did not want to mix with people whom they viewed as too far beneath their class.

An expatriate couple who had camping chairs in their living room, in a middle-class neighbourhood in Morocco, upset their neighbours because they lowered the standards on their street. Neighbours constantly questioned them about when they would purchase respectable furniture and curtains, and kept offering to help the wife choose something appropriate. In the same town, neighbours complained to a Western family when their habit of giving large quantities of food and money from their home brought numbers of beggars into the street. Money is usually given at the mosque, outside bakeries, or in public streets – not from the house. People prefer to give food from the home. A Moroccan proverb says, "Do what your neighbour does or move away from him." When we moved to a new home and upgraded our furniture, those poorer friends whom I thought might be offended or jealous commented that they were happy for us and still felt at home with us, because our house was always open to them. The poor still visited and the rich felt comfortable.

To buy good-looking furniture that we may not particularly care about, in order to make others feel comfortable, is not materialism. The choice is between spending money on what we value: comfort and convenience, or on what our host culture values: showing honour to the guest and self-respect. You do not need to be materialistic nor ostentatious in order to be honourable and give honour to the guests in your home. You do not have to spend a lot of money on the latest furniture either. Just notice what decorative touches locals use on the room where guests are received. Maybe you can afford something that will make a big difference to your home. When seeking to demonstrate Christ's love across class barriers, it is easier to reach those of lower social status than those above.

I have been writing for those Christians who err on the side of living too simply in a culture that puts a different value judgement on a good appearance. This tends to be more of a problem than Christians who live too extravagantly. However, being seen as too ostentatious is not appreciated by those in lower classes in either culture. A young Western missionary couple, sent by a wealthy denomination, arrived to begin their career in a Middle Eastern capital city. They rented an expensive house and immediately furnished it totally with brand new furniture from a chic company. This was carefully noted by the neighbours and talked about. Their lifestyle was the equivalent of that of middle-aged successful businessmen, but the husband was not seen to be "working" and was considered too young to be living off life savings. When neighbours asked what they were doing in the country, they explained that they were "here to learn Arabic". Neighbours wondered how young students could live at such a high level. The young couple explained that they had come to be missionaries, "to serve" with one of the local Christian Arabic churches. The neighbours talked with each other about it, as there was a mismatch between this couple's service role and their lifestyle. Some Muslims thought they were missionaries (this was voiced in muted tones), while others were sure they were spies. A local Christian said, "They must be millionaires." Their lifestyle did not make sense because of their age, status, and role in serving the church. Lingenfelter and Mayers describe Islamic societies at the "ascribed status" end of the scale:

> Islamic people will judge an outsider according to the rigid, dichotomistic standards of Islam, and according to his or her specific role among them.[1]

So what is wrong with simplicity? The problem lies in how the concept of simplicity is translated into Muslim societies. Ascetics are recognised in both East and West, but are expected to live in extreme simplicity. People of faith typically value a simple lifestyle. Probably most Christians would agree that it is a good Christian virtue to live simply, as opposed to living ostentatiously, or carelessly exploiting the earth's resources. And Christians would agree that it is a scriptural principle to avoid being ostentatious. Muslims may also be concerned about these same issues and have an ideal of a simple spiritual lifestyle. Sometimes, however, when we transplant Western styles of simplicity into Muslim cultures, they lack the proper signs of honour and dignity. Clothing can look frumpy, which indicates a lack of self-respect. Furnishings can look junky, which indicates the same, plus a lack of respect to guests. Simplicity is more a matter of contentment and a willingness to be poor or rich for God, and to holding material things lightly.

Men have discovered how important it is to wear a suit for business transactions and dealings with government officials. To wear jeans or casual dress will result in not being taken seriously, and could have repercussions such as a deal falling through or a visa not being granted. It denotes a lack of respect for the position of the official. In Egypt, a maid bought her Western employer's wife a pair of leather high-heeled shoes. She was embarrassed for this upper-class lady who wore heavy and dowdy-looking sandals in the street. The lady's footwear also reflected badly on her maid!

Western Christians often stand out in Muslim streets because they are not suitably dressed. Men tend to look too casual, which is viewed as undignified. In cities where women wear elegant fashions with jewellery, high-heeled shoes and a handbag, with the latest hairstyle, it is surprising to come across a foreign woman sauntering along in typical Western casual clothes, such as a T-shirt and jeans, or a full denim or peasant skirt and heavy sandals. To Muslims, she doesn't appear to care about herself.

Women openly snickered at an expatriate woman in Morocco for wearing sneakers with her *djellaba* (long kaftan-like robe covering the whole body which is worn outdoors). They could wear furry slippers, but sneakers were thought ridiculous. If you need to be comfortable while walking it may be better to wear furry slippers like your neighbour.

Having said that, I should mention that I have developed a hip problem that stops me wearing fashionable high-heeled shoes in a city where shoes are a fetish. I am aware of not being quite up to par, but that's life. So I am not suggesting anyone should damage their health, or their conscience, for appearance's sake; just be aware of its importance and put thought into it.

Jewellery is important. It is surprising how much jewellery Arab women wear; even poor women usually own more gold than Western housewives. It is an issue of financial security, but it is also a way to gain esteem, and a demonstration that their husbands esteem them. It is an issue of honour.

At marriage the groom's family gives a bridewealth to the bride, usually a set of gold (rings, bracelets and a necklace). Only in severely extenuating circumstances does a woman forgo this gift or give it up after marriage. Only the lowest of men would force her to give it up, or ask for the gold to be sold later in marriage, for example, to pay debts, without promising to replace it. In fact, a man does not have this right, as a woman's jewellery is her personal property and cannot be claimed by the husband, or by debtors, even if he is declared bankrupt. Women will voluntarily pawn their gold to help in financial crises, and cases are known where husbands have stolen it from their wives. Women who don't have a respectable set of jewellery will borrow from friends and relatives to appear appropriately dressed at weddings and similar functions. I have seen this happen in higher classes as well. For example, at a wedding the family wants all of its members to look presentable, in fact better than the new in-laws, so jewellery is lent to those who can't come up to scratch to impress the guests. Family honour is thus saved.

This is not to suggest that to live among Muslims you have to invest in a lot of expensive jewellery. We bought only rings when we married. I wore costume jewellery to social events as we kept our money for things that were more important for us. Women always assumed my jewellery was the real thing. When I told a close friend, who was not well off financially, that I had paid a few dollars for my gold look-alike necklace from a barrow stall in the marketplace, she was gleefully astounded. She warned me to keep it a secret and she would too. The jewellery was for private parties, not the street. Many pious Muslim women do not wear jewellery in the street at all. But the general word to describe everyone is "chic". Even in Saudi Arabia, women wear veils with the logo of Italian or Parisian fashion houses displayed in an obvious spot in order to gain status.

In most cities, women dress up to do the grocery shopping. A Western Christian woman in South-East Asia says: "It's a dilemma for me to figure out which nice dress and jewellery to wear to go pick up five kilos of potatoes at the market in 110 degree heat. But I have been doing it."

Appearance and response

Wearing the appropriate clothing makes a difference in how people respond to you. Western Christian families in rural north Africa and Gaza gained respect because the wives always wore the local type of veil. Actually, one wife in Gaza wore only a simple triangular scarf for a head covering, as one might wear to a picnic. Just the act of covering her hair in public was enough to weigh favourably with the local people. The wife in north Africa never left the house without wearing the same coverings as the Berber women. Once, while picnicking with his family in the mountains near their home, the husband got into conversation with another group of men picnicking nearby. When the men were told that this American family also lived in the town, they responded after some thought, "Oh, yes. We know they are a very good family. The wife always covers in the street." The conversation then developed along spiritual lines.

The men in Gaza and north Africa commented that they could respect the husbands' word because of the wives' discreet dress. The women's modest dress was so obviously different from the men's stereotypes of Western Christians that their barriers were broken down by the women simply walking in the street. The women's dress reflected the moral values in the home in a way that was understood and "proved" the husband to be respectable.[2] Local men understood that there was no danger posed to their families by being associated with this particular Western family. Their appearance spoke of shared moral and spiritual values with the Muslim community.

In Egypt in the past 30 years, women among all classes and ages have re-adopted various types of veiling. In the mid 1970s we saw the first urban women who re-adopted veiling appearing in the streets. It caused a lot of interest and comment from locals and Westerners alike. Thirty years later, on the streets of Cairo today, the majority of Muslim women are veiled. There are different factors involved, for example, religious aspirations, a desire to appear as modest as others, and pressure from family and society, but the one that I want to draw out is that appearance makes a point.

When we were living in Tunis, Khadra, a 40-year-old high school teacher, complained about people's odd reactions when she wore jeans on public transport. She sometimes wore jeans for private tutoring sessions with young children because she played on the floor with them. She often travelled on public transport and passengers were usually very polite, helping with heavy parcels and offering her a seat. However, when she travelled on public transport wearing jeans no one would give her a seat, or help if she was struggling with parcels. Many young girls wore jeans, but older women didn't usually wear them. She said, "I could fall flat on the floor and no one would give me a hand. I don't understand how people can react so differently to me, just because of my clothes."

While I was living in Morocco my father died suddenly. People I met in the street would give me the usual cheery greeting and then be embarrassed upon hearing the news. Then a Lebanese Muslim neighbour brought me her mourning veil that she wore to Christian funerals in Lebanon. So I adopted traditional Middle Eastern mourning. Even though it wasn't local custom, people recognised it, and complete strangers offered condolences and showed many kindnesses.

On another occasion, when my husband was having surgery in Bahrain, I wore the traditional *daffa*, a black cloak covering, in the hospital. While walking through a hospital corridor, a *daffa*-clad woman literally clutched me in her arms when I greeted her, and exclaimed, "She's Arab, one of us!" She took me into their ward where a niece was ill and introduced me to the other women in the family. We were reclining on cushions on the floor and drinking Arabic coffee. Suddenly, a male relative surprised both of us by climbing down into the room from a window to the outside. I was glad that I had not removed my *daffa* or it would have been embarrassing for both of us. We were introduced as if there was nothing unusual! Well, almost . . . he explained that coming through the window was faster than walking around the ward to the front door.

This was the root of the incident with our neighbour in Damascus. We had just moved into a new flat and all our neighbours were Muslim. One morning, Mazhar forgot something and returned home soon after he left, and rushed into the building. I heard a commotion in the stairwell: a lady complaining in a loud voice and Mazhar apologising. He came inside, looking flushed and embarrassed. Our neighbour, Um Fulaan, had been cleaning her front doorstep in the stairwell and Mazhar had suddenly come upon her and seen her without her head covering. Well, it seemed to me that if she didn't want to be seen without it, then she should not go outside without it. But that wasn't the logic everyone else worked by. Mazhar admitted that he should have made a noise to warn her that he was coming and given her the opportunity to go quickly inside. The final clinching argument was that since she was older than him, he should take the blame. And since I was a woman and she was a woman, I needed to go over and apologise again for him, explaining that he didn't do it intentionally and that he thought it was the same cleaning lady who had been cleaning the outside steps when he first left. She hummed and sighed and finally said, "Well, it's shameful because I'm a *hajji*"; by this she meant that she had made the pilgrimage to Mecca and was now extra careful. Mazhar should have treated her as if she was wearing her scarf!

In Egypt, I dressed in accordance with *hijaab* requirements (long sleeves and head covering) and this opened the way for spiritual discussions with women. In north Africa, women were complimented when I wore a *djellaba* and it opened up many opportunities for friendships. Complete strangers would talk to me and invite me home. Once, a young student at the language centre where I taught and studied politely told me, "Thank you for wearing a *djellaba*. It is a compliment to my country and our values when foreigners wear it." I was pleased that he had recognised my intention in wearing it.

On the other hand, a couple visiting in Yemen, who spoke Arabic, heard angry comments as they walked through the marketplace. The wife was dressed very modestly, and considered herself suitably covered, but she was not wearing a black street veil. They heard people muttering, "Cover her up!" The same thing happened with an American woman who lived in Damascus in 1991. She visited Hama and went without a scarf, as she did in Damascus, and heard people saying, "Cover it up!"

Wearing a headscarf is usually a sign of a devout Muslim woman, but in Tunis it brings problems. The authorities consider it a statement of Islamist leanings. In the 1990s authorities banned veiling in schools and forced students to remove scarves before entering campuses. Governors and mayors were urged to ban veils among civil employees if they wanted to be in good standing with the government. To wear any kind of head covering in the capital today is making a strong statement. It seems the only way for non-Islamist Muslim believers to show faith, without problems, is in conservative modest dress. One European woman was complimented by a local family for her appearance. She was a Christian and put thought into how to dress; she never wore tight pants, or pants without long jackets. The family were happy for their daughter to have a relationship with this foreign family.

Dressing for the occasion

Deciding how to dress respectably in another culture can be daunting in countries where there is a mixture of everything from traditional veiling to the latest Parisian fashions. Devout Muslim friends in Melbourne wear head coverings on certain occasions (when representing Islam at public lectures or meeting with Muslim clergy), and not on other occasions. The key for a statement of faith in dress is to be conservative according to the culture in which you live. This follows the guidance of Scripture to dress in a way that is "appropriate for women [and men] who profess to worship God".[3] Appearances are important. Muslims are making assumptions about us as we walk in the street. We are making a statement by the way we conduct ourselves and the way we dress. Respectable people care about their appearance in public and we will be judged by appearances. In some countries we need to *dress up* and be more carefully groomed, and in others we need to *dress down* and have less ornamentation or be well covered, in order to be respectable. What can you know about spiritual issues if people think you look unkempt, or even immoral? If you don't know how to look after your body, how can you look after your soul? I have found that I need to forgo personal preferences in order to be accepted as a mature, respectable person of faith.

The type of trousers men wear is often an issue. Jeans used to be unacceptable for everyone except students. But in some places they are gradually moving up into respectability in higher age levels. Slacks of any sort are often an issue for women. I noticed that some Moroccan women who wouldn't wear slacks in the street were perfectly comfortable wearing a swimsuit at the beach. I once saw a couple arrive at a local beach. The woman was riding behind the man on their motorbike. She was wearing the most traditional type of *djellaba* which included a hood and a face veil. When she alighted she began removing her clothes piece by piece until she finally got down to her itsy-bitsy French bikini. However, in most Muslim countries where it is acceptable to wear bathing suits at the beach, there are still many women who swim in their clothes rather than appear in public partly naked. All countries have a de facto dress code for different activities.

Although Hudson Taylor and his wife Maria, early missionaries to China, taught the importance of respecting local customs, in 1957 workers in OMF, the mission Taylor founded, were still learning the importance of dress the hard way. A young worker went to her first inland station and took all her prettiest dresses. She dressed in bright colours that were not worn in that area and in short sleeves when everyone else had long. Her senior worker attempted to suggest alterations in her wardrobe, but all were indignantly rejected. She plunged enthusiastically into children's work. One day her two favourite scholars did not appear and she asked her Chinese helper the reason. Their mother informed them that the children could not return. The missionary could not be a good woman because she dressed like a prostitute.[4]

In Sydney in 1972 I observed a heated discussion because the daughter of the pastor of one of the Arabic churches was wearing a sleeveless dress. The majority of the members silenced the man who had complained, by deciding that it was not yet an issue as the girl was only ten years old. It would have been an issue if she had been mature.

In Morocco in the 1980s an upper-class school teacher, who regularly wore Western dress, wore slacks on a picnic to the mountains. But to walk from her apartment to the car she donned a *djellaba* which she didn't remove until we reached the countryside. Other married, upper-class women wore jogging suits in their homes and donned a *djellaba* for quick errands by car or foot. Standards were more relaxed in the capital, and *djellabas* were not used as strictly as in the provincial towns. From town to town there may be different messages conveyed in dress styles.

All the latest fashions are visible today in Casablanca, and the woman in the story above might not wear the same clothes in the shopping malls in the capital as she would wear in a smaller town. Some Muslim countries are continuing to adopt more Western styles in dress, with tight jeans or spandex the norm. Silicone is normal where I live: Beirut has become famous as a destination for those wanting breast implants. There is typically a greater cultural difference between rural and urban areas in the same country, than in urban centres in different countries.

I have visited Muslim cities in north Africa, the Gulf, Asia and South-East Asia and there is a variety of dress within countries and within cities. It is impossible to make any rules for what is right for people of faith. One of my American friends moved from north Africa to a Pakistani area in England and discovered she was still keeping the same dress code in order to be seen as a spiritual and moral person.

Marie's husband works with the government in central Asia. Her local friends gave her negative feedback about how she dressed:

I have been taking another look at how I dress in daytime in public. In America, I often put on one set of clothes to wear all day long, to go shopping, visiting, to the doctor, or to stay home and do housework. Here, the people have frumpy house clothes for home and dressy clothes for public appearances. Then there is a third, very dressy set for special occasions. My daytime set is generally much better than their house clothes, but not as nice as their public clothes. In the past, I have worn my older daytime clothes to go shopping at the bazaar. The local women, however, wear their best daytime clothes to the bazaar. I think this is because it is often the only place where the clothes will be seen. It is a social occasion. You may run into a friend or business associate who needs to be impressed. I have discovered that it is not unusual for middle-income and poor people to eat only rice for months at a time, in order to afford a new dress or coat. Poverty is covered up. Walking with my poor neighbour to the bazaar I realised that she looked better than I did. She wore her nicest dress, and I wore my jeans pinafore and white shirt.

I do like to project the image that we consider spiritual values more important than material possessions. Still, I am now considering how to dress up my existing daytime clothes when I have to go to the bazaar. I have decided not to buy new things, but I will use the nicer things I already have more often. My newer clothes, combined with some jewellery, and hair pulled back in something other than an elastic band are improvements.

Appearance is a way of saying who you want to identify with and where you want to belong. When I dress in accordance with the local standards of decency I am trying to say to local people, "I like you. I like living in your country and I respect the things that are important to you." Getting it right can be a bit tricky, as my next experience also shows.

On a trip to Yemen I carefully followed local custom, wearing both slacks to cover my ankles along with a dress, and street veiling. The head veil I wore in Dubai was too transparent, so I purchased a heavier one. I was glad to discover that the women did beautiful henna-painting on their hands and feet in a similar way to Moroccan women. In Morocco, women were complimented that foreigners appreciated their art and beauty forms. I had my hands and feet painted by a local Yemeni artist. She was pleased with her work and felt complimented that I appreciated their customs. Walking in the street, totally covered with all my black veils, I noticed the henna was attracting undue attention and the women were giving it odd glances. I mentioned it to my American friend who had lived there for many years. As we were walking in the middle of the marketplace she told me, "Well, of course they are looking. It is sexually attractive. That's why women here wear gloves to cover it up." I walked home with scrunched-up hands.

In regard to men, sloppy clothes, or inappropriately long or short hair may cause people to write you off, and an earring may be a sign of homosexuality. If you don't see people wearing something considered normal in the West, there may be an important reason. Many devout men will not wear gold jewellery. Their wedding ring is silver. Traditionally, gold has been seen as a worldly metal, but not silver.

Our appearance could be telling people we don't know anything about life yet, much less about God and faith. There is an underlying issue of maturity. Traditionally in Eastern and Muslim cultures, age and wisdom are synonymous. Elders are to be given respect. Children are taught in the home and in school to respect and obey their elders. The proverb says, "He who does not act on the advice of his elder will have evil as his counsel." Younger siblings must show respect to the eldest son who will take the father's position in the family when the father is absent. For example, in one family a grown man would not smoke while in the presence of his father or elder brother. In many areas a son is not considered a responsible adult until he is married and has a child. The thinking is that young people do not have the experiences in life to be able to reach wise decisions like adults. Being young and therefore inexperienced in life is a disadvantage, usually only countered by education. In Morocco, people say of anyone who acts immaturely in dress or behaviour, "He still hasn't made any wisdom." Moroccans explain that this means, "Have mercy on him. He is just a kid. The time will come when he will understand. When he matures he will show more sense." Western Christians may be giving the impression that we need to grow into more sensible attitudes and beliefs.

Notes

1. Sherwood G. Lingenfelter and Marvin K. Mayers, *Ministering Cross-Culturally: An Incarnational Model for Personal Relationships*, Baker Book House, Michigan, 2000, p. 65.
2. 1 Timothy 3:1–13.
3. 1 Timothy 2:9.
4. Mabel Williamson, *Have We No Rights?* Moody Press, Chicago, 1957, p. 35.

person (Adam). Men and women were created of like nature and deserve mutual respect and honour. Family relationships are sacred, and special mention is made of revering mothers and honouring wives, through whom men come into the blessed experience of parenthood. Men are permitted to marry up to four wives simultaneously on the condition that they are all treated equally. They are to treat their wives with compassion, love and friendship (Surah 30:21). Women are to be paid bride-wealth upon marriage; this is somewhat similar to a modern prenuptial payment. This typically includes jewellery. These gifts remain the sole property of the woman and are not taken into account in the event of the death of the husband when assessing inheritance, and are retained by her in the event of divorce. Women are to inherit as well as men, but sons receive double a daughter's inheritance. This is because sons are responsible for all the women in the family. A son must financially provide for his mother and sisters as well as his wife.

Marriage is the norm and is highly esteemed, as the family is the basis for the new people of God, so behaviour which threatens the family unit, like adultery, is not to be tolerated. Any aberrant behaviour is to be rooted out, as it weakens society. Adultery and homosexual behaviour should be punished. Casual sexual relationships are forbidden, as they weaken the sacredness of the marriage relationship and the family. Men are women's protectors because they are physically stronger and they are obliged to provide for their wives' total financial needs and emotional needs. They should treat their wives kindly. Marriage should be a place of mutual respect and honourable intentions. The wife has the right to be clothed, fed and cared for by her husband. Wives should be obedient and supportive of their husbands and guard their virtue and their husband's reputation and property. Great importance is attached to womens' proper behaviour, because this is what holds the fabric of pious society together. Decency, kindness and justice should prevail in all relationships. The husband's reputation hangs on his wife's behaviour, just as the community's honour is invested in the behaviour of its women. In family quarrels the husband is given the right to use coercion, including physical "chastisement", to restore order (Surah 4:34). This is interpreted in different ways and to various degrees.

> The duty of the man to command his wife is embodied in his right to correct her by physical beating. . . . The right of correction, which was thought likely to be used to excess by husbands, was restricted by the Prophet (who was very kind to his wives) to "decent" proportions.[1]

However, if the wife is physically abused she can be granted a divorce. In addition to this, if the marriage does not work out for reasons of incompatibility it may be terminated by divorce. How easily a woman obtains divorce depends on which country she lives in and how negatively her family view divorce. In most Muslim countries only men have the right to an easy divorce.

These regulations are understood by many Muslims to have been socially progressive and need to be understood primarily in their historical context. They actually were favourable to women and provided better treatment than they were receiving in pagan societies. In those days female infanticide was practised. Daughters were not as valuable as sons, and newborn girls could be left outside to die. So the reminder that men and women both came from Adam is giving value to females. Wives could be simply cast out, so new inheritance laws were ensuring provision for women so that they could not be cast out destitute. Allowing four wives put a limit on men's practice of taking numerous wives. And the requirement to treat concurrent wives equally and provide for each one in the same way was a discouragement to polygamy. It was also a time of war and there were a great number of widows and orphans without the means to exist and polygamy provided for these destitute women. The marriage bridewealth gave women some independent means. Accusations of adultery had to be backed by four witnesses who actually witnessed the act. Men's guardianship of women was to protect them as the weaker sex and wives offered obedience to their husbands out of gratitude for their care.

The Islamic world today is facing the problem of how to interpret these laws in modern life. Should they be literally enforced, or should the spirit be followed in new ways in a new age? How these laws are enforced or lived out in families today differs from country to country and family to family. Strict literal interpretations limit honour to women mainly in their roles as wives and mothers, and do not allow them self-determination and access to life in the public sector. We saw an extreme example under the Taliban in Afghanistan where women were denied any access to public life, and modest and chaste behaviour meant veiling from head to toe and staying in the home. "Rebellious" women were beaten or executed. Most Muslims are against this interpretation, claiming it is not true Islam, nor in the spirit of Islam. In another strict regime, that of Saudi Arabia, women are not allowed to drive and must totally veil in public. However, they do have access to education, employment and public life because there is total segregation of the sexes. In many countries women can choose whether to veil and whether to work or stay at home.

Veiling was instituted as the means for freeing a Muslim woman to take part in public life, while remaining modest and not revealing her body in an inappropriate way. So we see the former prime minister of Pakistan, Benazir Bhutto, leading her country, yet always covering her head in public. Islam teaches that women should keep their bodies modestly covered. The Quran tells women to cover their bosoms and the other body parts that should be covered for religious reasons of modesty. This typically means covering areas considered sexually stimulating to men. Many women cover their hair, throat, chest, legs and arms. But ideas about what is modest tend to run along cultural lines. Pakistanis, for example, are more concerned about covering ankles than arms, while many Arab women will be more concerned about covering upper arms than ankles. Chinese Muslims may be more careful about wearing socks than a headscarf. Some women are very positive about veiling and proudly choose it as an expression of faith; some women are forced to veil, either by family or government; and others are totally opposed to it. All are Muslim views.

Modesty is not just a matter of dress. It is proper behaviour, befitting the people of God. Muslims generally keep a greater distance between the sexes than is usual for most Westerners. Some may not want to kiss, or have eye contact or any tactile contact at all with persons of the opposite sex, believing this kind of contact could lead to moral temptation. People with very narrow interpretations believe this contact makes them ritually unclean. When it is appropriate to kiss the opposite sex, it is on the cheek, never on the mouth. This is a totally personal matter and it is impossible to generalise. It does help to be aware of this issue when meeting Muslims of the opposite gender. Generally, Muslims will tend not to offer to shake hands with the opposite sex until they see that the other person is willing to do so.

There have been many women leaders in Islam since its earliest days. There were women taking significant roles in the days of the prophet Muhammad who discussed, questioned and struggled with the new lifestyle being mapped out for Muslims; these included Aisha, Khadija and Sukaina. There have been women warriors leading men into battle, women mystics leading men into a deeper union with God, women poets and feminists, and women in every area of secular life.

Today's women

In most Muslim countries today, women take an active part in public life. They participate in higher learning, graduate with prestigious degrees, and pursue careers in every field, including government. At the same time, Islamic cultures differ from Western culture in that parents may still take an active part in choosing who their children marry or what they study or whether girls work. We will look at some examples later on.

At the same time, some women have experienced oppression. The Islamic community acknowledges this and is addressing this issue and there are a number of feminist movements. Women are more likely to be oppressed in the poorer and un-educated classes.

It is interesting to Westerners that while Australia and the United States have not seen a woman leader, a number of Islamic countries have had Muslim women leaders, for example, Pakistan, Bangladesh, and Indonesia. This is actually because they are hierarchical societies, and a woman from a high-status family relies on her status more than her gender. Muslim societies are usually high-status societies, so status ends up carrying more weight than gender.

Muslim women complain that Western Christian women pity them, without understanding their beliefs and lives. Randa was born in Sydney, studied and graduated with a law degree in Victoria in 2001, and speaks for Islam in the media. She writes,

To some people my identity as a Muslim meant that I was either a terrorist, or an oppressed Muslim female who couldn't speak English, form an opinion, or work a remote control. My identity is continually challenged in university. In between encouraging us to come to pub crawls and "Bachelor of Intoxication Dinners", university hosts were boasting about their acceptance of diversity. I was excluded from nearly all the orientation activities not because I was unsure of myself, but because I was confident in myself. I gradually found the courage to think only of my destination and nothing in between. I soon came to realise that with that sort of courage God will reward you with a good deal of meaningful "in between" anyway. I've come to realise that I know myself as a young Muslim woman not in spite of the stereotypes that exist about me, but because of them. I've been inspired to understand the hyphens of my Australian-Muslim-Palestinian-Egyptian identity, and have found that my journey through spirituality has given me strength, pride and independence in my celebration of my God-given rights and my acceptance of my responsibilities towards God, myself and others.

Women take an active role in community worship and have their own area set apart in mosques to pray. They tend to have a smaller presence in mosque prayers than men, with many women preferring to pray at home.

A church in the USA invited the local mosque community to a home for a meal together. The Christians asked men from the Arabian Gulf why their wives had to veil and why many did not work. The men responded, "Our wives are precious and we respect and protect them. We prefer they stay at home to care for the family rather than face daily stress in the workplace. If we can afford to support them, why should they work? We are not oppressing them. We are protecting them."

Muslim feminists would disagree with these men and argue that women do not need protection, but encouragement and self-determination to realise their full potential. Where is the boundary between protection and domination?

Western Christians struggle over how to live in Muslim societies when faced with such divergent attitudes to women and among the women themselves. Do we follow the conservatives and, if so, how does this fit with our belief of personal freedom in Christ? Or do we follow the feminists? Then we must ask how much it is appropriate for guests in a country to challenge the moral and religious foundations of its society. If we decide to challenge our hosts' beliefs and customs then we had best be sure we understand what we are challenging and why. The host doesn't usually appreciate the guest changing the house's furniture unless it is the host's idea. The issues of women are not just a problem for women. How will a man treat his wife and family and other women? We will return to this important question later when we talk about the family.

Muslim women as role models

As guests in Muslim culture we can learn from our host's behaviour. Muslim women emancipationists understood how to work within their culture and many chose to follow a scriptural principle to "put themselves under the law in order to free those under the law".

Wafa Sunien, who became a minister of parliament in Syria, explained the strategy of the political union members to attain their goals. They carefully lived within the limits of the "old habits and outworn traditions" of the things they were trying to change.

> In retrospect I can see that this was very important. . . . Thus, in a very short time we started gaining people's respect and admiration.

There was a price to pay of course. We had to look more reserved in our appearance than ordinary women. . . . Although my political affiliations and intellectual ambitions were unorthodox, we remained well in line with acceptable traditions.[2]

Nadia Nouhid, a Lebanese journalist and author of *Candles*, a feminist book, writes:

We give too much importance to social opinion and . . . women end up paying the price. When you appear and dress respectably [men] can't help respecting you. . . . We have our morality, traditions and ways of thinking and we should try to keep our character rather than be lost in futile attempts at imitation [of the West].[3]

Queen Nuur of Jordan is an example of a Western woman breaking down the barriers, gaining a good reputation, and influencing society. First, she gained status with a capital "S" by her marriage to the king. But she also cultivated her image by publicly conforming to the conventional roles. She consistently stated that she was not influencing the king in politics. Her domain was the home and the social side of their responsibilities.

In contrast to Jehan Sadat of Egypt, who enraged Egyptians (and other Arabs) by overstepping traditional boundaries and "interfering" in politics, Nuur carefully guarded her public image. She appeared with sleeves and carefully groomed hair or head coverings in traditional areas. On the other hand, Jehan Sadat brought a storm of criticism on herself when she went to Saudi Arabia and appeared bareheaded. Even Queen Elizabeth of England and Queen Sofia of Sweden wore specially designed hats when they visited Saudi Arabia. Mrs Sadat totally overstepped the line when a daily paper published a photo of her allowing herself to be kissed on the cheek by foreign heads of state. All classes of women were outraged by her "improper behaviour", which reflected on her husband's popularity. Colonel Gadhaffi of Libya had giant posters made of THE KISS and posted them in the streets and at the international airport in Tripoli. In 1991 an upper-class Muslim lady, who was a lecturer at the American University of Cairo, one of the most progressive and pro-Western elements in society, told me that she was still personally affronted by Madame Sadat's behaviour ten years after the event: "Muslim women don't behave like this." I can only speculate on how much Madame Jehan's refusal to submit to conventional standards of behaviour contributed to her husband's assassination by the Islamists. She was becoming a "wild Western" woman, typifying her husband's "open door policy" to the West, which Islamists believed was leading the country into degradation.

Queen Nuur carefully submitted personal desires to a higher calling. She said in an article that she could no longer live to herself and must always be careful to remember that she represented a royal family and a royal kingdom. Everything she did or said reflected on those whom she represented. She gives a reminder to Western Christians that what we say or do reflects on the One we represent.

Notes

1. Fatima Mernissi, *Beyond the Veil*, Indiana University Press, 1987, p. 111.
2. Bouthania Shaaban, *Both Right and Left Handed*, Indiana University Press, 1988, p. 56.
3. *ibid.*, p. 106.

CHAPTER FOUR

LIVING WITH VEILS

Historical Muslim and Christian veiling

Christians veiled before the coming of Islam. From ancient times, respectable dress for Eastern women involved veiling, and continues to be so in many countries today. Respectable Greek and Roman women covered themselves in the street with a large veil. This is evident in sculptures and paintings, where the veil is often draped around their bodies as a shawl. In north Africa, where the Romans colonised the northern parts of these countries, the northern women still wear a large white veil similiar to the one worn by Roman women in sculptures left in the area. By contrast, in the southern areas (where the Romans did not penetrate) women wear the original colourful, classic Berber dress, without a white body veil. In Palestine in the first century, women wore long garments reaching to the feet, and a head veil. The head covering was usually worn over a stiff cap on which coins, the woman's bridewealth, were sewn. The present-day Palestinian peasant costume follows the same style. My husband remembers his mother wearing this type of headdress in Syria.

Veiling was considered a necessary modesty for Christian women in the first century. The old Roman Catholic nuns' habit carries on the tradition in Western Christian circles. However in Arabia, beyond the scope of the Greco-Roman empire, women did not practise veiling until the prophet Muhammad's wives were obliged to veil, and all Muslim women adopted veiling.

The Quranic injunction to veil states:

> Tell your daughters and wives and the believing women that they should cast their outer garments over their persons when they go abroad; that is most convenient that they should be known and not molested. (Quran 33:59)

Yussef Ali's commentary on the text reads,

> The object was not to restrict the liberty of women, but to protect them from harm and molestation under the conditions then existing in Arabia. In the East and West a distinctive public dress of some sort or other has always been a badge of honour or distinction, both among men and women.[1]

Under Assyrian law, low-class women, slaves and prostitutes, were forbidden to veil as "honourable" women, and were severely beaten if caught outdoors in a veil.[2]

Veiling was an upper-class privilege and it appears that in adopting it, Muhammad desired to give public honour to his wives. In the early years of Islam, as countries came under Muslim domination, non-Muslim subjects were penalised: their women were denied respectable public dress, and were forbidden to veil. Veiling came to be associated with the privileged Muslim upper classes, particularly during the Ottoman empire when a face veil was included, and veiling was generally thought of as a principally Muslim custom.

Muhammad Nasri Al Din Al Albani quoting early Islamic law states that early Islamic rulers put conditions on the Ahl-Aldhema [non-Muslim subjects under Muslim domination]. Their wives must not dress as honourable Muslim women. They must wear clothing that exposes their legs and must not cover their heads.[3]

Over time, this rule was no longer enforced and non-Muslim women under Muslim rule re-adopted veiling in order to escape harassment on the streets. But the pre-Islamic roots of the veil were forgotten and it came to be associated exclusively with Islam and abhorred in Christian circles. An American journalist, on a visit to a Palestinian family of the Orthodox Church in Jerusalem in 1896, writes,

We commented on the circumstances that the izzar – a square white sheet tucked and banded about the figure – is worn by women of all nationalities and religions in most cities of Northern and Southern Syria [current Syria, Jordan, Lebanon and Palestine]. It is a Moslem custom and we marvel at the adoption of it by Christians. [Her Christian host explains:] "Many years ago the Christians – Greeks, Romans and Catholics alike – were accounted as nothing by their masters. The Christians did not care to muffle up their women and hide their faces, but they were forced to do as the Muslim women did, to save their wives and daughters from insult when they went into the streets. So they fell into Muslim fashions in this and in other things, and even now must wear the izzar [sheet] and mendeel [face veil] in public."[4]

Women continued to wear the veil in many Middle Eastern countries until the early 20th century. William Barclay, the renowned Biblical expositor, has important points to make about the veil in his commentary on 1 Corinthians 11. There are different Greek words for the English translation of "veil" or

"head covering"; to read the text with these distinctions gives
us this Arabic translation:

> Every man praying or prophesying with a head covering dishon-
> ours his head. But every woman who prays or prophesies with her
> head uncovered dishonours her head for that is one and the same
> thing as if her head were shaved . . . (11:4) For if a woman does not
> completely veil herself [wear *hijaab*], let her also be shorn. But if it
> is shameful for a woman to be shorn then let her be completely
> veiled [wear *hijaab*].[5]

As Barclay continues,

> The problem was whether or not in the Christian church a woman
> had the right to take part in the service unveiled. We must remem-
> ber the place of the veil in the East. In Paul's time the Eastern veil
> was even more concealing. It came down right over the head with
> only an opening for the eyes and reached right down to the feet. A
> respectable Eastern woman would never have dreamed of appear-
> ing without it.[6]

Eastern churches are still discussing whether a woman should
worship unveiled. In 1992 the following article appeared in an
Arabic daily paper, titled "Christian Veiling (*hijaab al masi-
hiyaat*) in Egypt."

> The case of moral Christian dress has become important to the
> Copts after Archbishop Musa, General Director of Coptic
> Theological Higher Studies and Education, wrote an article on the
> topic in the Coptic magazine WATANI published last Sunday
> under the title "Modest Dress for Women". He was answering the
> question, "What is understood by modesty for the Christian
> woman? Is modesty required inside the church building only or
> outside as well? Is modesty satisfied by just a scarf or shawl cover-

ing her head during communion, even though her clothing is tight and naked, or seductive?" The Archbishop Gregorious replied in his article, "Modest dress for a woman must properly cover her body and must not be tight fitting showing her shape beneath. The material must not be too fine showing her body through it. Also it is not proper for modest young girls to appear in the street with naked arms and legs. And especially in worship in the church a woman must cover her head with a scarf or a face veil or a shawl."[7]

In Sharqia, a suburb of Cairo, Muslim and Christian women wear identical veils in the street: a long black tent-like dress covering the body, and a head covering. In areas where this type of veiling continues to be practised, Christian women are still required to wear their veils in church. (In other urban suburbs of Cairo, veiling may not be an issue, but the congregations, including evangelicals, sit segregated. I attended a Coptic service in Sydney, Australia in 1972 where the congregation sat segregated.)

What is the relevance of the Corinthian passage when we are living in societies where women still veil and would not leave the house without it?

Women who were activists in social work with AMAL, the Shi'ite military and social movement in Lebanon, and who bravely confronted the Israeli occupying forces, testified to the importance of "decent" dress in their leadership roles.[8] Um Mohammed Biadon, head of the Women's Movement of Southern Lebanon, who formed groups in which women were educated and trained to rebel against the unfair conditions, says,

I wear Islamic dress when I need to go out and mix with men. . . . Basically Islamic dress is holy. I don't like to be treated as a female body. We all know if we lift our sleeves a bit the men are going to concentrate on our hands rather than what we say. I want my brain rather than my body to speak for me. In society I want to behave normally and move freely. It is not just a matter of clothing. It is exemplified in voice and movement too. *Hijaab* protects the family and protects the woman from being viewed as a sexual object.[9]

I have been criticised for wearing Muslim dress (by Christians in Egypt and by unveiled women among my in-laws) and for not wearing it by Muslims. We were at a Muslim Sufi group's weekly gathering. I had been observing how the women dressed and noted there was not a consensus. So I wore an outfit I had specially made for religious occasions: a slack suit with a knee-length jacket and long sleeves. I took a scarf with me in case all the women happened to be wearing head coverings that day. They weren't. In fact, when we picked up one of the women from her work she came out in an almost sleeveless dress. In the street, in front of the sheikh sitting in our car, she put on a three-quarter-sleeve blouse – and no scarf. I decided it was inappropriate for me to wear a scarf. Two other women came, both wearing *hijaab*, strict veiling. That put me in the middle, more covered than one, less covered than two, and I thought this was a good place to be.

After the meeting, one of the veiled ladies criticised me for not following Quranic dress, "particularly in the presence of the sheikh". I produced the handy scarf and explained, and offered to wear it for their sakes in future, as it wasn't a problem for me either way. "You shouldn't do it for others, but for your own conscience and God" was her reply. The sheikh and the other veiled woman, Fatima, came to my defence, mainly explaining that "she is obeying her book". That gracious statement placed me on the other side of the religious divide. Fatima then complimented me on my modest and beautiful dress. But the lady continued complaining about people who do not obey their religion and veil: "The Quran says . . ." At this point I surmised she may have been really speaking to the unveiled Muslim woman through me.

The dynamics of this group were very interesting. The upset woman was a known TV personality. After involvement with this group, and due to her deepening spiritual life, she adopted veiling and only accepted suitable TV roles. The unveiled woman whom we had picked up at work had previously been veiled, and had worn a lot of make-up and jewellery. As a sign of deepening spirituality, she had removed her make-up and jewellery, and the veil. I discovered all this when Fatima drew attention to these changes, showing how each person is being responsive to God's leading in their own way. The group had a dynamic understanding of individual response to the spirit and motive of religion, rather than the rules and law.

Some Christian women object to veiling as an Islamic custom. But history and Scripture show us that the custom has its roots in Eastern conceptions of decency, not in Islam. And what about our witness if we Westerners are viewed as the ones bringing moral corruption to their society? Surely this passage has a literal contemporary message. For myself, in countries where most women still wear a street veil, I wear the all-enveloping body veil, without the face veil.

Paul told women in these situations, exemplified in Corinth, not to remove their veils in case their freedom was seen as licence and the reputation of the church was damaged (see 1 Corinthians 11:16). He urged women to respect the social customs of their time, in spite of their new-found freedom. The reason for Christian women to veil in these strict societies is that our Scriptures recommend being culturally sensitive. So I would still have been following my own book if I had decided to veil in that Sufi meeting. What stops me from suggesting that this is a blanket statement to veil in Muslim societies is the fact that it is speaking to women who are already veiled. For a woman outside the society to adopt veiling is different and could be giving a different message. Veiling may not always be best, as this woman's experience describes:

> My husband teaches at an Islamic university in a country area of Indonesia. That is the reason I decided to wear a head covering. From day one, everyone loved it. I am a tall, blonde, blue-eyed lady, so there is no way of hiding my foreignness. Women nod in approval to me or tell me I dress well. Tourists get hassled at the market a lot, but I have never been hassled. I have always been treated with utmost respect. Other foreign ladies keep telling me how rude the men are; yet young men politely greet me.
>
> However, the rule of covering is not a blank "covering is best". One time we were travelling to the capital and I walked off the boat at the first port. The large crowd of local women all laughed in my face.

There are popular stories told of Muslims who follow Christ and totally renounce their former religious and cultural traditions. Women who found a new liberty and joy in Christ expressed this by dramatically overthrowing their past customs. They removed their veils, cut their hair short, and cut their dresses off at knee and forearm length. One woman who did this spent long periods away from home attending Christian meetings. Her family was shocked and perplexed by her behaviour. She told them boldly of her new faith in Christ, but they assumed her absences and loose behaviour meant she was carrying on an illicit relationship. Their shocked reactions were largely due to her throwing away conventions and respectable customs. It is very difficult for a faith testimony to carry weight if the first sign of new faith is perceived to be immorality or rebellion. She began receiving threatening phone calls, and suspected the family was behind them. In this case, many people tried to discourage her from such radical actions, but to no avail. She later came under persecution from the authorities for her faith. The police interrogating her, and others connected with her, pointed out her appearance as a sign that she was on a downward moral path.

Many Muslims will not consider investigating Christ, because they think discipleship involves turning their backs on family and community values in favour of Western individualism, rejecting a monotheistic faith for polytheism, and abandoning strong moral traditions for morally lax styles of Western behaviour. This is not the Gospel.

In Muslim countries today, head coverings still relate to decency, submission to God and authority. This story comes from a Western Christian living in Morocco in 2003:

I have been teaching an English class in my neighbourhood for several years. Recently, our landlord's daughter joined the class. She is a conservative Muslim who wears the street veil and headscarf. She said she was interested in joining our class, as opposed to someone else's English class, because she knows I am a woman of prayer and that I follow God. I was surprised to hear this because she lives in a different neighbourhood and has only met me a few times. I wondered how she had formed her concept of me. Eventually I remembered she came to the baby party for my son, held three and a half years before, in our home. She heard me tell the story of how we initially were unable to conceive and that my husband prayed with me in the middle of one of my despairing nights, and we went to sleep in peace. And finally, some months later, we started having children.

Repeatedly, I have also heard other neighbour women at parties telling guests about how I wear the headscarf and street veil. They also talk about my good deeds and kind, egalitarian attitude toward people. Although this isn't necessarily what we Westerners would consider sharing the good news, I've learned that for Muslims here, it is a great step forward in the right direction. They see our outward appearance first and then our actions spurred by faith. Having visited the villages of several friends who now live in the city, and the more I understand the culture here, I do not go out without covering my head anymore. The scarf is symbolic of my modesty and my respect for conventions and fear of God.

Long hair has a sexual symbolism in the Islamic world and is seen as a temptation for men. Hence, religious women are careful how they wear their hair in public. Long hair is not left free. Girls explained the significance of hairstyle with this Arabic proverb: "She is running around unrestrained, as loose as her hair."

However, even though I have advised women to follow local norms, we need to realise that the crux of the matter is not in the dress itself – what type of dress, or veil, or no veil. The issue is the meaning of modesty and what particular context determines the use of veiling. The Western Christian woman learns these things from local women. It is a matter of "seeing sexually": does the sight of this piece of anatomy excite the opposite gender? As Christians we affirm sex as something blessed and given by God. We do not play loose with it or deliberately flaunt ourselves to attract the opposite sex. In societies where women's main avenues for advancement are through men, or where they are economically tied to men, women dress to attract men. In a redeemed culture, based on kingdom values, men and women will try not to cause the other sex to lust. They will adopt appropriate behaviour and dress.

National identity and women

When leaders in Muslim society began reform movements to lead their countries into democracy, they set women's emancipation as the first step and heart of the reforms. Many of these nationalist movements were in response to colonial occupation by Western powers, such as Britain and France. Since then, the Muslim world's struggle for identity continues to affect women's emancipation directly and this has a see-saw effect on modern and Islamist attitudes to women's place in society and to their dress. We need to keep in mind that women's liberation occurred during our friends' mother's or grandmother's time. In some countries there have only been two or three generations since women left the harem and seclusion. There has been a cycle of veiling and downveiling, as society responds to the issue and women are caught in the pendulum swing between modern and traditional values. Many have lost their moorings. Abla, a Syrian grandmother, comments, "The equality [women] have achieved has become a burden to them because of the many new responsibilities it has brought with it."[10]

Emancipation began in Tunisia in the 1950s.

By the mid-1960's official and unplanned pressures for social transformation had set in motion a psychological and cultural revolution. So far as women were concerned this meant that educational and professional opportunities were expanding, that substantial numbers of well-dressed, unveiled Tunisian women could be seen on the streets on the major cities, that men and women could be seen working together in business establishments and public acceptance of all these phenomena was growing. Because of these changes, Tunisia acquired a reputation as the Arab state in which women were making the most progress.[11]

But full emancipation in Tunisia coincided with the arrival of the miniskirt, and the country began experiencing a reactivation of tradition, with the government's approval.

> In 1969 President Bourghiba gave a talk that signalled the change in his outlook. He discussed the need to put modernization in perspective; and referring to women's emancipation, formerly one of his most cherished goals, he warned that too much reform will lead to a loosening of morals. Freedom must be coupled with religious and moral education in order to produce the respect for virtue that was formerly assured by long robes and heavy veils.[12]

Women in the Muslim world are juggling the responsibility that freedom brings. Western culture is still in the same struggle and many are beginning to worry about the negative effects on the family of the clash between autonomy and obligation.

Women's emancipation is an issue that is connected to past colonialism and fears of Western domination. A veiled Egyptian woman says,

> Before colonization women dressed like this. It was the Europeans who imposed their way of dressing on us. We want to go back to rediscover our identity. We want to abide by the rules of modesty.[13]

New resurgent Islamic groups that are against Western influence are making women's role in society a political platform. Women in Egypt (and other Middle Eastern countries) have voluntarily returned to traditional patterns of dress. The Western model is seen as detrimental to the moral core of society. Women are trying to find a balance between freedom, keeping honour as it is still understood in society, and loyalty to Islam.

Some Tunisian women are returning to Islamic veiling in spite of strong opposition from the government, which is afraid of the Islamist movement. Egyptian and Jordanian women have not left the workforce, but have adopted veiling in order to participate in society outside the home. They want self-determination, but they also want it with traditional respect and dignity. They consider that in adopting the West's style they have lost valued esteem. In Egypt,

> Veiled women have capitalized on the ambivalent feelings and insecurities men have toward Westernized women. The veil became an advertisement for virtues, the old-fashioned yet still valued attributes of modesty and good reputation. The veil makes possible the desired combination of education and income without the connotation of immorality Westernization carries.[14]

During the 1980s, Kuwaiti society was breaking down because so many women had abdicated their traditional role and left the running of their homes to foreign nannies and house help. A woman minister in the Department for Public Health and Nutrition said that the nation was raising a generation of obese, malnourished children because the mothers were not supervising their children's diet. The family unit was disintegrating, husbands were dissatisfied, and polygamy and divorce were on the rise. Women leaders in Kuwait issued a unified plea: "What happened to the perfect wife and mother? Where is she? Women, please go back to your homes; the nation needs you."[15] There are reasons behind this plea that can appear to be simply a cultural preference for larger families. Most Muslim societies are pro-natalist. This preference links with nationalist aspirations: the nation needs larger families to provide more persons for all the categories of society; it needs more soldiers to defend the country, more political party members, etc. So this plea connects to historical, political and economical reasons.

Modern invisible veils

One of the boundaries between the sexes is speech. It is important to learn what subjects are appropriate for discussion in mixed company. All subjects connected to a woman's personal life and grooming are among the topics that are taboo in mixed company. Some Western cultures do not consider these things inappropriate. Unfortunately, I have often been in situations where Westerners have talked about these subjects in the same way that they refer to the weather, and have embarrassed those present.

In some village cultures the women will not even refer to an obvious pregnancy in front of the male members of their families. In an Egyptian village, while sitting with the entire family, I asked a bulgingly pregnant young wife when she was due to deliver. She was so embarrassed she turned bright red and couldn't speak. Her husband and father-in-law suddenly found the sugar cane growing outside the window intensely interesting and turned their heads, pretending they didn't hear anything. Usually in cities there is no problem about referring to a pregnancy. On the other hand, a Western woman was surprised by the boasting about sex that occurred sometimes in mixed company in a Kurdish village. Take time to learn what is appropriate. These subjects are issues connected to honour and respectability.

Names can be a form of segregation. First names are not used in many parts of the Middle East. One of the signs of the importance of sons is that parents are called by the name of their firstborn son. For example, the wife is known as "Mother of Ziad" (Um Ziad), the name of her eldest son. The father is called "Father of Ziad" (Abu Ziad). Husband and wife use this form of address in the presence of others. Even among the same sex, people use the title of "Um So-and-so", not their pre-name.

In Australia, in the 1970s, Syrian Christian friends took me to visit another Arab family. After we left I asked for the wife's name. They had been friends for three years, but didn't know her name. It was totally baffling to me at the time, but after living in the Arab world I understand why. She was "Mother of so-and-so", and no one had needed to know her name. However, in Beirut, right next door to Syria, personal names are used. An American friend who moved from Damascus realised she didn't know her friends' names. She had ignored pre-names when introduced and had instead asked after their children, making note of their firstborn's name. But later she noticed that they all used first names. She is too embarrassed to ask their names after such a delay and is hunting for clues.

In many countries a man should not even ask his friend, "How is your wife?" He should enquire generally about "those in the house". Men must learn that the women's world is not their business. They should feign ignorance and stay on their own side of the veil. It is difficult for Westerners to understand the proper boundaries between the sexes. After the September 11 attack, there was some subsequent hostility towards Muslim communities in the West. A church in Melbourne offered to help the local Muslim community by taking any veiled women shopping who wanted public security. The problem was that they offered the services of men! Presumably, they thought the women would feel safer with a male escort, and didn't realise it was equivalent to offering to take out the men's wives on a kind of date.

Notes

1. Abdullah Yussef Ali, *The Quran: Commentary and Translation*, Dar Al Fikr, Beirut, 1987.

2. J.B. Pritchard, *Ancient and Near Eastern Texts*, Princeton University Press, 1955, p. 183.

3. Sana'Al Masri, *Khalf Alhijaab*, Sinai Publishing House, Cairo, Egypt, 1989, p. 98.

4. Marion Harland, *The Home of the Bible*, Bible House, New York, 1896, p. 218.

5. William Barclay, *The Daily Study Bible*, 1 Corinthians 11, Arabic edition, Dar al Thaqaafa, Cairo.

6. William Barclay, *The Daily Study Bible: Letters to the Corinthians*, Westminster John Knox Press, 1993.

7. *Al Quds*, 16 December 1992, p. 4.

8. Bouthania Shaaban, *Both Right and Left Handed*, Indiana University Press, 1988, pp. 84, 98.

9. *ibid.*, p. 87.

10. *ibid.*, p. 38.

11. Lois Beck and Nikki Keddie, *Women in the Muslim World*, Harvard University Press, 1978, p. 145.

12. *ibid.*, p. 147.

13. Wedad Zenie-Zeigler, *In Search of Shadows: Conversations with Egyptian Women*, Zed Books, London, 1988, p. 80.

14. Elizabeth Fernea, *Women and the Family in the Middle East*, University of Texas Press, 1985, p. 69.

15. *AlSayidditi* (Arabic magazine), London, 1987.

CHAPTER FIVE

LIVING WITH STEREOTYPES

Wild, wild women

We owned a wonderful piece of junk when I was little. It was a wind-up gramophone that played tiny records. We owned two records and one was "Cigarettes and whisky and wild, wild women". I have met many Muslims who think those lyrics describe modern Western women. A number of Muslim eman- cipationists mention that the Western woman is seen as a threat to the sanctity and morality of Muslim family life. Fatima Mernissi, from Morocco, says that fears associated with the destruction of the traditional Muslim family and the condition of women are justified.

These fears embedded in the culture through centuries of women's oppression are echoed and nourished by the vivid and equally degrading images of Western sexuality and its disintegrating family patterns portrayed on every TV set. It is understandable that Muslim husbands and fathers feel horrified at the idea of their own family and sexuality being transformed into Western patterns. . . . It is worth noting that these fears are not totally unfounded; the

nascent liberation of Muslim women has borrowed many characteristics of Western women's way of life. The first gesture of liber-
ated Arab women was to discard the veil for Western dress, which
in the thirties and forties and fifties was that of the wife of the col-
onizer. . . . Another factor that helps in understanding men's fears
is that the Westernization of women has enhanced their seductive
powers. The Muslim ethic is against women ornamenting themselves and exposing their charms; veil and walls were effective
antiseduction devices. Westernization allowed ornamented and
seductively clad female bodies on the streets.[1]

Engelbrektsson, in a study on the effects of immigration on a
Turkish village, states:

While abroad, many of the men have been in close contact with
European women, even on intimate terms, a fact which most of
them boast about. Many of the men appear to be enticed by the
idea of having a Western type woman for a sex partner. Yet much
of what they find exciting and thrilling about Western women as
companions in fun and sex are attributes which they would never
accept being displayed by their own women. In the eyes of the men,
the emancipation of Western women has created disorder in family
life and in society as a whole, and has resulted in ways of behaviour
on the part of the women which are not morally acceptable for
decent women.[2]

I have found the above quotes to be a typically Muslim stereotype of Western women. For example, I, and other Western
women married to Arab men, have had identical experiences in
being introduced to Muslim friends and family. A look of surprised relief comes over their faces. Why? What were they
expecting? After registering this typical reaction to me, one lady
burst out, "Oh, but she's so feminine, with soft clothes and long

hair and holding a baby and all!" Maybe she was expecting a wild, whisky-drinking woman, or someone out of the raunchy Western TV serials shown widely in the Arab world.

Muslims typically confuse Western with "Christian", and Muslims have told us they believe that Western soap operas are true depictions of the Western Christian family: free sex, wife-swapping, addictions, and dishonest business dealings. In a group for couples in cross-cultural marriages in Cairo, one Egyptian husband said that colleagues had shown scepticism about his Western wife and had openly asked how he controlled her sexual behaviour. He responded by telling them that she was not out of *Dallas* and did not need controlling.

Christians normally believe in chastity and confine sex to marriage. To us, it is not OK to be promiscuous and this makes us kind of bizarre Westerners. This story comes from Oman:

> When I first got to know my Omani friend, she mentioned in passing that Christians don't need to get married in order to have sex. When I explained that wasn't true, that Christians were supposed to wait until they got married before sex, she was shocked. She said that the Asians (working as house maids) "all" say that "they are Christian, so it doesn't matter if they walk 'naked' in the street". She has told me several times over the years that since meeting me she defends Christian morality and tells her friends that those people walking around "naked" and doing all those things on TV are not following their religion.

The following is an unusual story and will shatter some stereotypes. I had a 19-year-old girlfriend in north Africa. She had no faith, although her family was conservative. She often declared that she would never allow herself to be "held back by this rigid society". We usually defended her parents' values and shared their concern. Although they did not seem cognisant of her behaviour, they complained about the obvious signs of loose dress etc. and were suspicious enough to send her younger brother around with her to keep an eye on her. She often seemed able to elude him and on one such occasion called on us, while a young American man was staying with us. Since we were not home, and he didn't understand local customs, he invited her in to wait for us. In the short time that they were alone, she asked him to sleep with her. She was genuinely shocked that he refused, and she later told me, "But that's what everyone does in the West! That's what freedom is!" As her story unfolded, we discovered that she had already had two abortions and regularly slept around with different partners without any kind of commitment. She gave credit to her sixth-grade primary school teacher, a Frenchwoman, for leading her into what she called "emancipation". She eventually left north Africa and went to France. We were quite worried about what sort of life she could be pushed into if she arrived without any employment, and we tried to dissuade her from going.

A few years later, a well-groomed young woman arrived at our front door. It was our friend, who had married a Frenchman. Her husband and father-in-law had travelled with her to meet her family, but she was too afraid to tell her parents. So the French family were hidden in a hotel. She broke the ice by telling her parents about her girlfriend, who had done the same thing. They were scandalised that her friend had married an "immoral Christian infidel and wrecked her life". The girl then became afraid that they would forcibly detain her if they knew the truth. She stayed about a week, with high drama running between our house, her parents' house, and her French family's hotel room. She introduced us to her husband and father-in-law who were good and caring people. We offered to be go-betweens but she was terrified. In the end, she decided to wait until she had children and then inform the family "so it would be harder for them to break the marriage". The three went back to France, mission not accomplished. She could not face the power of the family's stereotype of immoral Western Christians. Actually, none of them mentioned anything about faith.

Stereotypes and reality

"This is what people do in the West." What should be our reaction to this accusation? We could react like some missionaries in rural Egypt. When a new missionary wrote to these missionaries requesting advice on what type of clothing to bring, she received this reply, "The Muslim women wear long skirts, so we wear short skirts." Or we could ignore local customs, like the group in the Arabian Gulf who offered hospitality to two married male visitors; they were assigned a flat with two single non-Christian women, sharing a common bathroom. Comings and goings would be visible to local people. The men declined the accommodation and stayed in a hotel.

Or we could make an effort to respect local customs. Conservative Muslims' sense of right and wrong is more acute than that of Western Christians. In spite of the fact that we consider ourselves to have a strict spiritual/moral worldview, we are surprised to discover that conservative Muslims do not view us as a spiritual people because of our behaviour and dress. Clothing is an important, and necessary, way to make a statement. If you live in a Muslim community you will notice the different clothes used for weddings, circumcisions, mourning, and to show religious affiliation. Actually, it is not just Muslim custom, but Eastern: Hindus, Buddhists and Sikhs and Eastern clergy also use clothing to tell a story about their spiritual life. In the West we expect clergy to wear distinguishing signs, but not necessarily the laity. When Muslim women develop religious aspirations, one of the first and most notable ways they show this is in their dress. Local people often asked me why I dressed so conservatively for a Westerner, and many enquired if I was a Muslim. I usually told them that the Bible teaches that godly women should dress modestly, and since I have submitted my life to God through Christ, I want to be modest in their country as well as my own. So, if they recognise godliness and decency by a certain type of clothing then I will wear it while in their country. I have been asked if I wear a scarf in Australia. I answered, "No. A head covering generally has no religious meaning in Australia. Australians only wear scarves if their ears are cold. But I do wear modest clothes. Christianity does not give us laws, but principles that can be applied differently in different places." Since multiculturalism has replaced Anglo-Saxon culture in Australia, this statement needs to be unpacked a bit more. Head coverings ARE the norm for veiled Australian Muslims!

From my observations, in most Muslim countries women have ways to show they are simply being modest or making a definite religious statement. Usually the key sign is the way they wear their scarves. Devout Muslims tie their scarves tightly around their faces so that no hair is showing at all. There are communities of Western converts to Islam in Muslim countries which carefully adhere to prescribed Islamic lifestyle and dress. While I want to appear modest in Islamic society, I do not want to deliberately give the false impression that I am a Muslim convert. This is a difficult balancing act and there may be better ways to solve it than I have found. Actually each country or area within a country may need a different solution. In Egypt I tied my scarves in a loose way that revealed my hairline, and I often wore a visible necklace with a cross. This gave mixed messages. But at least people recognised that something a bit different was going on, that I wasn't a typical tourist, and they asked me to explain.

In the Arabian Gulf there has been an influx of poverty-stricken young women from eastern Europe coming for prostitution. Many wear the *abbeya* (black cloak covering the body). Moreover, I discovered one of the ways that young people find to circumvent rules of segregation involves loose head veils. When girls are passengers in cars and see desired young men as the cars pass, they surreptitiously slightly lower their headscarf. The guy gets the message and throws in a phone number. (Young people spend hours in telephone and internet conversations or flirtations.) So a foreigner wearing an *abbeya* with a scarf showing hair is more likely to give the message that she is available, than that she is a devout person of faith! In the Gulf it seemed simple for me, as I was with my in-laws and so dressed as they dressed: full veil and full scarf. We all wore scarves inside the house as well. Veiling is not necessarily a sign of oppression or passivity or backwardness. Two of my young women in-laws who dress this way are at university. One is studying medicine and the other civil engineering. I need to tell you that they were not the ones responsible for my discovery of the head veil ploy. They are very respectable and have no contact with men other than relatives.

Anatomy

The key question is our interpretation of modesty. I have seen enough Christian women in the street "naked" to realise that we have some ignorant thinking about standards of decency and what Islam terms naked. I use "naked" in the cultural/religious sense of showing parts of the body that ought to be covered. Nakedness is defined differently in different cultures. Did you know elbows can be really sexy? Showing the neck or forearm or ankle may be considered a shocking display of nudity in other cultures. If we want to be respectable then we need to know what decent and indecent dress in other countries is. I have seen some Christian women in conservative countries, where most women wear a veil, appearing in the street in shorts. The Western equivalent would be to go out completely naked. A tribeswoman may be completely modest wandering around in the jungle topless, but she had better cover her breasts if she visits New York.

Buttocks are seen smouldering under slacks. I have deliberately used suggestive language to try to portray how buttocks are viewed across the Arab Muslim world. Breasts, arms, face and legs are usually considered sexually stimulating, yet within that culture on certain occasions they may be benign; for example, when nursing a baby the breast may be completely exposed in mixed company with no shame. In some places, Muslim women still bare the breast to nurse in public, while modestly keeping their faces veiled, or their calves or upper arms covered. But buttocks are never benign! In a scene from a Middle Eastern TV comedy the boss is commenting on his beautiful secretary. She got the job because she has the best credentials. She slinks across the room and we see a screen full of her credentials: fleshy buttocks swaying from side to side! Notice how the men in the coffee shops intently stare after the women who have already passed them. They are not straining to see the back of their heads.

Arab women who are deliberately being seductive show it in the way they walk by an exaggerated movement of the buttocks. Tight skirts and pants give added effect. In Morocco, women wanting to attract attention pulled their silky *djellabas* tightly under the buttocks as they minced along. Thus by enhancing the buttocks, a garment designed to cover physical beauty is turned into a means for sexual attraction. In Turkey, a progressive young woman from a leftist background arrived for dinner dressed in tight body pants and a sweater barely covering her buttocks. With most of her movements the sweater rode up and she was continually engaged in pulling it back down in place. This small action is often observed as women walk in public places: the little tug to ensure a sweater or jacket is still hanging properly and is not caught up.

The traditional Arab preference for well-rounded women has a long tradition. It appears in the classic work *Risaalat Al Ghafraan* by Abu Alala Al Maa'ri, written in the tenth century AD (405 H). Al Maa'ri, an anti-religious philosopher, using witty sarcasm, ridicules Islamic leaders through a fictional character, Sheikh Ibn Qaarih. Ibn Qaarih is speaking with two relatives of the prophet Muhammad: his uncle Hamza and his son-in-law Ali. The sheikh is drawing an imaginary picture of the material riches in paradise. While he is prostrate in prayer, one of the young women of paradise appears in front of him. She is thin and unappealing, so does not deflect him from prayer. But then she turns her back and he sees her well-endowed "other" view, and he breaks into praise extolling her beauty. He likens her seat to "sand dunes in the desert", a thing of beauty for a Bedouin. However, no other part of her anatomy is mentioned. We expect to hear something of her beautiful eyes, or lips, or gossamer hair, but apparently this lady had only one good attribute. Until early in the 20th century, heavy women were still highly desired as wives. The heavier the girl, the greater amount of gold was bestowed on her father at marriage. A number of Arabic colloquials still use the same word for "healthy" as "fat", meaning "beautiful". Although perceptions vary from place to place, and in different areas within a country, I have not yet come across anywhere in the Muslim world where buttocks are not among the most sensual parts of a woman's body. I think this Arabic cartoon sums it up:

From *Strange and Amazing Women in Ancient and Modern History* by Said Sadiq Abd AlFatah (Publisher: Madbouli)

A touchy subject

Western women regularly complain that they are touched, or grabbed, while walking in the street in some Muslim countries. I am not suggesting that it is a problem peculiar to Muslims. My sister was pinched black and blue while touring Rome, and finally retreated to her hotel room without seeing all she planned. On the same trip, when she visited us in inland Morocco, it never happened once. However, Fatima Mernissi, a Moroccan sociologist, explains that the traditional Muslim thinking is that women in male spaces are considered both provocative and offensive. Since schooling and jobs both require women to be able to move freely through the streets, modernisation necessarily exposes many women to public harassment.[3]

She relates the findings of a survey which revealed that rural young men believed that any women walking in a city street were sexually available.[4]

So if it happens, how to deal with it? Don't accept it. I once hit a man with a stick, and people in the street congratulated me. Men who do these things shame the rest of the society, and others in the street will, or should, act on your behalf. Locals have advised screaming and pointing out the offender. Nearby shopkeepers would then pounce on the offender and beat him to a pulp. I heard a story in which two ladies were walking together when one got touched, and she did just that. When the shopkeepers beat the man up, the lady was very alarmed. Her companion consoled her, saying he deserved it. She responded, "Yeah, but they got the wrong guy."

A Syrian Christian man suggested to Western women that violence and name-calling are not really appropriate responses for Christians. He said that we should simply say, "Respect yourself!" Women found that worked very well. But one woman commented that, as a male, he has never had to face the problem!

This well-thought-through response comes from a Christian woman living in north-west Africa:

Let me first note that I have met many honourable, polite and friendly Muslim men, who know how to show others respect. However I also had a few bad experiences with inappropriate behaviour.

In our first year (1985) in a rural area, I was twenty-three. I was wearing the veil, as I always do, and a high school boy approached me and grabbed at my chest. I was horrified. I just went home and cried on my husband's shoulder.

A short while later, a man approached me in the street (again I was wearing the veil from head to toe) and asked if I wanted a man. It was obvious from the look on his face that he wanted to know if I wanted to sleep with him. Again, because I was still new to this town and did not know the language well, I did not know what to say. I went home and asked my husband how I could say "You are a pig!" in the local language. I can laugh at it now, but at the time it was very upsetting.

On a few occasions I have received lewd remarks from a man or men in a shop and my husband was near enough that I could go and report the incident to him. He went and shamed the man in question, calling the man's action cowardly – to have affronted a woman in that way. He challenged the man that if he had anything to say to his wife that he should direct his remarks to him and not to an undefended woman alone.

I am interrupting her letter here to draw attention to an important point for men. Never, ever, let such an incident go unchallenged if you are on the scene. Touching a woman does not only damage her honour, but her husband's or father's honour. It is a situation that must be addressed. Think of it in terms of an old-fashioned challenge to a duel to preserve the good name of a lady and family. It is a direct insult that must be addressed in order to keep one's honour. Think how men are viewed who refuse to take up the challenge. Note the husband's remark to the local man about having anything to say to his wife in the street. Of course he should not have anything to say to a strange woman in the street; he should not be noticing a veiled woman. The point of a veil is to allow women to pass invisibly through public spaces (men's domain).

The woman continues her story:

We also have to use our powers of observation to see how honourable women in the local culture deal with these problems. We can also ask a number of different locals how they would handle it. Another recommendation is to take off your shoe and hit the offender with it. The kind of shoe doesn't matter since the main point is to shame the man by being hit, or even just struck at. Often just taking off your shoe and showing the sole works very well. This more specific action will also help bystanders know exactly who the offender is. It doesn't take long for folks to get the idea that even "foreigners" don't like this kind of activity. Many think they can get away with it, and they usually do, because the shocked lady doesn't know what to do. Given that men do not touch local women in the same way, we do not appreciate this treatment. We must let the offender know that we don't like it. The man usually claims innocence: "I didn't know foreigners don't like it."

In a related incident I was walking past a mosque near a militant group's training centre. A young man with a beard and a certain kind of turban stopped me in my path and began cursing me and spitting in my face. Thankfully the Holy Spirit came immediately to my aid and I simply wiped my face and began out loud to bless this young man, saying things like "May God bless you and give you long life. May He open the way of truth to you. May He give you well-being." The young man was so shocked by my reply that he just stood there with his mouth hanging open and then I quietly walked away, saying as one often does in parting where we work, "I commit you to God, with peace." On another occasion when I was sitting out in front of our home, a militant type yelled at me in the street for wearing the veil, saying that as a Westerner and a Christian and a blasphemer I should not be wearing it. (The large majority of the local people love the fact that I wear the veil.) Again the Holy Spirit came to my aid and reminded me of a local proverb which we quote often which says, "Whoever enters the woods sings the song of the birds." It's their equivalent of "When in Rome do as the Romans." Again the man was silenced and all his companions laughed at my witty reply, which broke the tension of the moment.

Looking back on these encounters and some others I've had since then, I am just reminded how many preconceived misconceptions we have to face in the Muslim world as Westerners. We have to go the extra mile to overcome these preconceived ideas so as to remove as many stumbling blocks as we can. So I think that we need to do all we can to learn from the people how to live in their culture as insiders, with an understanding of their language and their culture, so that we are better equipped to handle the many challenges we face. We also need to ask God to give us help in every situation to have the right words and the right response.

God's design is equality for the sexes. The West has unhealthy gender value systems and Muslim culture has unhealthy gender value systems. My advice is to be sensitive to the culture, because it is helpful for your relationships. Muslims should see that we Christians are different from their stereotypes of Westerners. We make a statement of our spiritual aspirations, or lack of them, by simply walking down the street.

The Western church's approach to gender has been challenged by society, and many Christians have rediscovered healthy models in ancient Celtic Christianity.

The Celts did not, like our society, oppress women, repress femininity, or emasculate men. Women had different roles, but equal status. Sex, like everything else in the physical world, was positively embraced as something God-given.

When God is in the centre, sex becomes sacred. The meaning of sex is the deep desire for intimacy, connection and creation: it is interwoven with the desire for connection with God. That is how we learn about love. Once we try to unweave these things, then God, love and the sacredness of sex are lost.[5]

Notes

1. Fatima Mernissi, *Beyond the Veil*, Indiana University Press, 1987, p. 167.
2. 'Women left behind: a case study of some effects of Turkish emigration' by Ulla-Brett Engelbrektsson, in: Bo Utas (ed.), *Women In Islamic Societies*, Curzon Press, London and Malmo, 1983, p. 234.
3. Fatima Mernissi, *Beyond the Veil*, Indiana University Press, 1987, p. 143.
4. *ibid.*
5. Ray Simpson, *Exploring Celtic Spirituality: Historic Roots for our Future*, Hodder & Stoughton, London, 1995, pp. 80, 82.

CHAPTER SIX

LIVING WITH SEGREGATION

I knocked again at the door. It looked the same as the doors on all the other houses in that street in Melbourne, but it acted weirdly. Someone behind it yelled at me. Then the curtain moved slightly at the window and I glimpsed someone look at me through the crack. Still the door didn't open. I wondered how many people in the street were watching me behind their curtains. For their benefit I opened my handbag, pretending to be absorbed searching for something. There was another female yell, but I could not hear what the voice said. I figured it must be saying "Go away." What else would anyone yell through a closed door? My new friend Muna, a 22-year-old Arab Catholic, had given me this address. Maybe it was wrong? I turned around and headed for the road, feeling like an unwelcome intruder, and with growing indignation at the door's rudeness. Suddenly the door flew open and there was Muna with a big smile. She called me back, telling me she was very glad I had come. I returned to the house very confused.

Many years later: the bell rang and I opened my door in Beirut and found an elderly man, who had come to visit my husband. I informed him that Mazhar was not at home, but would return very soon. I expected him to say he would return later. He stood at the door. There was an awkward moment of inaction and silence. He broke it by asking the question that caused all the trouble, "Can I come in and wait?" There was another moment of awkwardness. I can only recollect a man asking me this question twice in 25 years in Arab countries. Both times I said "No", and neither decision was easy. This time I tried to calculate what the elderly man was thinking and if there was some cultural cue I was missing. First, he was old enough to be my father and I am not young either. Did he consider us beyond gender boundaries? Would I be insulting him by implying he was sexually unsafe? Second, maybe he just needed to sit down and didn't have the energy to walk to the next coffee shop and wait. How could I be so lacking in compassion? On the other hand, maybe he was one of the more rigid Christians who refused to sit in coffee shops, because he considered them worldly places. Where else could I suggest he sit? It was unthinkable to suggest such a dignified old man sit on the concierge's chair in the stairwell. And what would I do if I allowed him in? It would be very uncomfortable. Should I seat him in the living room, but leave the front door to the stairwell open, and kind of ignore him? Or should I serve him drinks and treat him according to the usual rules of hospitality – but then not return to the room, and leave the front door open? Would that be acceptable? Did Lebanon operate on different rules than the other countries I knew? I ran out to the balcony, hoping to see some sign of Mazhar in the street, with no luck.

After agonising over it, I apologised that I could not invite him inside and gave custom as the reason. It seemed ridiculous to be reminding this old Arab man in his own country that his custom was the problem. As I feared, he was very insulted, and left, declaring he would never return. I was concerned I had done the wrong thing, until Mazhar returned and we discussed it. Mazhar discovered that the man was a Christian who had family living in our building. In fact, when he left my place he went one floor down in the lift and sat with his family. When Mazhar went to visit him to sort out the situation the man confronted him, "Your wife insulted me. What she did proves you are Muslims. We have free access to each other's houses. I felt like I had done something wrong. You are not believers in Christ."

Opening the door can be a very complicated situation. In my story a Christian Arab came to another Arab house. He was met by a Western Christian who did not act according to Western custom, or according to Arab Christian custom in his circle. I operated according to the custom of my Muslim in-laws and the wider Muslim culture of West Beirut. Other Arab Christians we know would have done the same as me. On the other hand, there are some Muslims who would have invited him inside. Maybe I should return to the custom I saw years ago in Melbourne, and when someone knocks at my door, without opening it, yell loudly, "Who's there?"

Soon after this incident, an old friend visited from Morocco and we talked about what was going on with doors in his country. He said, "Traditionally, the man answered the door so as not to expose his wife to men and thus save the problem of honour, even the extreme of killing her, if she was exposed to other men. But the custom of men answering the door is changing, with women having access to public places and travelling alone. Often it's a woman who comes to the home to borrow something. The generally accepted rule of thumb now is that the woman answers during the day, when men are supposed to be out of the house at work, and the house is the woman's domain. The man answers the door at night."

A problem of perspectives

In the Arab world, there are no "babies" born, only "male" babies and "female" babies.[1] For Westerners, the world consists of *people* and we tend to relate to *people* asexually. But in Muslim societies life is gender-based. The world is essentially male and female. An Eastern woman doesn't speak to a person when she addresses a man; she speaks to a male person, and her behaviour alters accordingly, usually keeping a slightly more polite distance.

People watch us and are quick to judge by appearances. While I was living with a local Christian family in Jordan, there was an enormous row between the mother and daughter-in-law. The young wife sold yogurt through the local shop. One day a customer needing some urgently came to the house to buy it. She refused to sell from the house, and he left. The conversation lasted about five minutes. Later, her irate mother-in-law berated her loudly, over and over, for being alone with the man at the front door for an inappropriate length of time. She said that she should have just said "No" and shut the door in his face – which sounded very rude to me! Years later in Morocco, a man mistook our house for another. When I answered the door and he discovered the mistake, he inquired about the family he was searching for, and then left. I turned to find my irate husband demanding to know why I was chatting to a strange man in public view at the front door.

Egyptian friends in Cairo were very careful of their reputation. Whenever male relatives or couples visited them the husband always put in an appearance on their balcony to make sure neighbours knew he was home. People are suspicious and they gossip. We are too naive.

Sexual segregation in all its forms is an evidence of the power and importance of sexuality. Muslim women are concerned to keep their sexuality from interfering in their dealings with men. The following statement by a Muslim woman may be an exaggeration to make a point, but it does show us a different worldview. She said, "We all know that when we raise our sleeves, men will concentrate on our hands rather than on what we say." I don't think that it would occur to many Western women that arms could be a turn-on.

Women and men worldwide use voice inflection to show interest in each other. What we need to notice, in Muslim societies, is that if you use the same cheery greeting for both your neighbour and her husband, you could be giving the spouse of the opposite sex a different message. When speaking with the opposite sex you need a cooler manner. Westerners tend to be a bit naïve about this, but Muslims are aware of these boundaries. So are Eastern Christians. Hence we have all the unwritten rules about how to screen sexuality: avoid lengthy eye contact, adopt modest postures, watch the tone of voice, keep your general demeanour more reserved. While we should be effusive and affectionate with our own sex, we need to distance ourselves from the opposite sex by being cooler to them than we would be with Westerners.

Families control the sexual activity of their members because it has the greatest potential for disrupting family unity, because of its link with the family's honour.

> In the final analysis, the separation of the sexes, the pretence in front of the young that sex does not exist, and the value placed on sexuality as a signature of family honour all merely confirm its supreme importance. Sexuality, in short, is affirmed through constant denial.[2]

What does segregation look like in daily life? This description from South-East Asia could be from any Arab country in homes where it is practised:

We were invited to visit a family where my husband had previously visited. He told me that he had never seen the wife. She was always behind a curtain. Whenever the drinks and snacks were ready, he would hear a knock behind the curtain and his friend would go and bring out the refreshments his wife had prepared. Immediately, I pictured a woman who was fully veiled apart from her eyes. I couldn't but help wonder, how will this relationship develop?

We were welcomed by the man into his in-laws' home. He then directed me to a room behind a drawn curtain. I went through the curtain and that was the last time I saw my husband till we went home. I was greeted by three conservatively veiled females – the wife, her mother and her 11-year-old sister. To my relief, I could at least see their faces. The wife was busy cooking in the kitchen so her mother beckoned me to sit at the dining table. The little sister was busy helping prepare two sets of refreshments – one for their one female guest and the other for the men in the living room. Every time the sister had refreshments for the men, she would carefully place it underneath the curtain and carefully push it through to the adjacent room. Her father would then take it from the other side.

The wife was very friendly with a lovely jolly disposition. I soon learnt that she and her four siblings had all gone to a religious school for their formal education. When I asked her mother why she decided not to send them to the state school, she explained: "We believe that when we die, God will ask us how we raised up our children. I want to do it well." The wife was eager to know how I converted to Christianity. All of them listened with interest. It was interesting to me that she understood it needed to be my decision and not something I was born into. As I got to know them better, I realised their genuine desire to please God. To them, this includes wearing the veil. To wear the veil in the heat is not a burden to them, but just one of the many ways to obey God's laws. As I left the home that day, I realised that the wife was very much unlike what I had imagined her to be. She was a very happy and contented woman.

Of course, I think she is still missing out on a special relationship with God through Christ.

The ambivalence of woman's sexuality still prevails in the culture.

Mediterraneans have traditionally believed that a male could not possibly suppress the strong urges that take possession of him every time he is the presence of a pre-menopausal woman. . . . And women are considered even more unable to resist males.[3]

In some traditional literature woman is portrayed as evil. She has a strong sexual drive which she cannot, or does not want to, control. She is sometimes portrayed as a source of moral danger for man, and deliberately flaunts her charms to bring him to disaster. The unabridged version of *A Thousand and One Nights* is pornographic in parts. Its morals are attacked by modern Arab writers (for example, in *The Dreams of Scheherazade* by Taha Hussein).

In some Muslim countries to this day, a woman is still considered legally and morally unable to be responsible for herself. Therefore, she must have a guardian (*wali*) for the course of her whole life, to take responsibility for her. We watched a popular Egyptian soap opera, *Married but Strangers*, which portrayed the incongruous plight of a successful businesswoman unable to attend a meeting abroad, because her husband would not give his written permission for her to leave the country. The authorities carried out his order to prevent her from leaving the airport.

This image of woman as dangerous is intensified when applied to Western women, who are free of the restraints of traditional society to control their behaviour. We have listened to

Arab friends discussing the Western woman as someone who is more sexually free and therefore dangerous. This supposed wild, whisky-drinking Western woman, without personal or social restraint, must be a veritable virago in their minds! Electrifying currents flash between the male and female worlds, but we Westerners wander through, blithely unaware, because we simply see *people* and attempt to relate to both sexes in the same way.

As we now know from the above stories, in Muslim culture men do not usually enter the house when the husband is not present. This was the first problem with Rosemary and Mustafa in our opening story. He expected to be asked to return when Tom came home, but Rosemary warmly invited him in, and opened the door to lurking stereotypes. Arab culture assumes that there is only one reason why a man and woman are alone. Whereas, if sex entered Rosemary's mind at all, she probably did not want to insult him by implying that he must have sexual intentions, knowing that Muslim culture is very conservative about sex. The prophet Muhammad is attributed with saying, "Whenever a man and woman are alone, Satan will be the third person present." Society will assume the worst. A lost reputation cannot be regained.

Cleanliness is next to godliness

Another problem of perspectives is the way in which Muslims and Christians may denigrate each other. Muslims have told me, and others, that Islam is the best religion because it is the "cleanest", based on Surah 10:54, and that Christians are "dirty". They mean this in its literal sense. There is a collective memory passed down from centuries ago when the Western crusaders were discovered to be below the standards of local

Muslims' personal cleanliness; they were dirty. On the other hand, Western missionaries in the early part of the 20th century, in these same areas, describe the Muslim populations as suffering from "unsanitary conditions, dirt and neglect".[4] Both Muslims and Christians link the cause with each other's religion.

Muslims wash numerous times a day. Apart from normal bathing, they perform ritual ablutions five times a day and wash after marital relations. Water is always supplied in toilets, as paper is not considered clean enough. Part of children's religious studies at school is learning how to wash after certain activities and regain ritual cleanliness. Arab women remove all excess hair because it is considered unfeminine and "unclean". Circumcision, which is prescribed for all Muslims boys and is related to the Abrahamic covenant, is also "cleaner".

This personal cleanliness crosses over into washing their homes. It's typical for women to wash floors twice a day. Even though the house is cleaned daily, the women will also dust the living room immediately before expected guests arrive. Eating utensils are typically washed under a fully running tap and rinsed numerous times before being pronounced clean. Most shops and many houses are "cleansed" by incense first thing in the morning.

Muslims in the West have told me that they are nervous about eating in Western homes because the food may not be "clean" (*hallal*). They will travel long distances in order to obtain meat killed in the *hallal* way: according to the Quran; this is the same as the Old Testament law requiring no blood in the meat. Some Muslims are concerned about eating from kitchens or plates contaminated by "dirty" pork. It is good to inform Muslims that you never have pork in your house, if it's true. Think how you would feel if you suspected that you were served food on a plate that was shared by the dog: washing it won't make it feel clean!

Deadly gossip

The English ditty "Sticks and stones can break my bones, but names will never hurt me" is just bravado which everyone knows is not true. Name-calling does hurt us, but a lost reputation can kill in some countries. Rumours about a woman's sexual misconduct can lead to her being killed by her family to regain the family's honour. Bouthania Shaaban describes witnessing an honour killing in her village in Syria in 1968, in which a young man who had just killed his sister walked through the street waving a dagger dripping with blood. When he reached the police station to hand himself in, he yelled loudly for everyone's benefit, "I've killed her and saved the family's honour!"[5]

I know families where male relatives have killed, or tried to kill, one of their women to regain honour. A Muslim girl and Christian man fled Egypt to marry overseas. The girl's father ordered her elder brother to kill her. When he refused, the father ordered his son out of the house until he obeyed him. He then lived with some students and was a broken person.

In Syria, suspicions about a wife's adultery were "confirmed" when she was seen in discussion with a man in the street. She was killed to save the family's honour. In Jordan, a Christian girl was found to be having an affair with a Muslim married man. His family beat them both severely, leaving her permanently crippled. Years after the event, when I was their neighbour, her uncle arrived one night, drunk and carrying a shotgun. He loudly shouted his intention to clear the family's name by killing her. Neighbours intervened and prevented him from carrying out his threat. Since I only lived in that area for three months, I wondered how often this event occurred.

But did he really want to kill her? People are expected to lose control in certain situations, and persons in the vicinity should supply the restraining force. In north Africa a teenage girl made a habit of slowly walking home from school with some boys. Her father was very strict and went ballistic when he found out. She was compromising herself in finding a marriage partner and ruining the family's good name. He yelled and screamed in a rampage around their house, threatening to kill her. The girl barricaded herself in her bedroom. The mother was the inter-mediary trying to calm him down, but he worked himself into a frenzy and totally lost control. He grabbed a kitchen knife and began battering the bedroom door, making a lot of noise, but not much of a dent in the door. It was time for group inter-vention. The mother raced to a neighbour, calling for help. The father was so enraged that no reasoning or pleading made any difference. The only way to regain honour was "to kill her".

The neighbour lady now used shock tactics: she embraced the father, locking his arms and the knife, and telling him to calm down and forgive the girl. Suddenly, he was brought back to earth, and was embarrassed at finding himself in a bear hug with his neighbour's wife. The situation was under control. The neighbours all confirmed that they knew they were an honour-able family. They told him they knew his daughter was innocent of anything terrible: "We all know what a good girl she is. She's just young; forgive her for our sakes." The girl is still alive, but she stayed in her room for over a week, with her mother sneak-ing up food.

Widespread honour killings are making headlines around the world. They are practised by both Christians and Muslims, as evidenced by one of the above examples. (The practice is also found in some other religions.) It is a vestige from the old tribal life. Many locals are against the custom, but one of the problems they face is that they are seen as lowering moral standards. The implication is that if you are against honour killings, then you are supporting sex outside marriage.

The family's honour, which is the most important factor in society, is vested in the women. In the West, the typical definition of a "virgin" is a male or female who has not had sexual intercourse. In Arab culture it is a female who can prove it, if needed, by a doctor's examination. The woman's life could hang in the balance of this proof. The family may kill the woman simply on the basis of a lost reputation, without needing proof. Gossip literally kills in these societies, and avoiding causing gossip is a controlling factor in behaviour. It is typical for brothers to escort their sisters as chaperones until the girls become engaged. One brother, from a very strict family, said it was less trouble to chaperone his sister now than to be forced to murder her later!

The law has a special category for these killings. It may not be codified, but it is understood; it takes into consideration defence of life, property and honour, and gives a more lenient sentence than for murder. I asked two Arab lawyers if part of the leniency is because of the understood guilt of society. First, society demands the killing, and second, society did not intervene to prevent it. One lawyer confirmed the idea, but it hadn't seemed to occur to him before. However, an Arab Christian minister said that this is giving too much generosity to the culture, and that the lenient sentence is just another way that women are oppressed, as there is not an equivalent practised on men.

As Christians, we should be totally opposed to this custom. We have a story in the Gospels where Christ saves the woman from being a victim in an honour killing: the woman taken in adultery. Jesus rebukes the men for their double standard and restores the woman, with a warning not to commit the sin again. The problem today in Eastern traditional society is that there is no way to acknowledge that sex outside marriage is wrong and, at the same time, forgive the person and restore her to society. While we need to stand against this custom, Christian men need to be careful that they do not get local women into trouble by inappropriate behaviour: engaging women in conversation in the street or, in particular, laughing in a carefree way in the street. When local Muslim men friends pass me in the street, they give a brief head nod of acknow-ledgement, or a curt greeting, and nothing more.

Honour and space

This story comes from an American man living in the capital of Jordan:

> I decided that I would try to honour one of my wife's single, con-servative friends. When she knocked at the door, I would leave my wife to welcome her in and sit in the living room with the doors closed, so that I never saw them or even heard their conversation. One day she told my wife, "Your husband is a very honourable man; not like [another American husband] who always invites me in, shows me to the living room, talks to me, and brings food in when his wife and I are talking." I tell this story to Western men so they realize that "what seems best and most logical" to us is not always the best way to be honourable in this culture.

In social settings people try to sit next to their own gender. So they play a kind of musical chairs so that same sexes sit together. They take note of what seats are available and how they are distributed between the guests in the room, and choose appropriate seats. In plain language they are uncomfortable with a man sitting next to a woman on a couch, unless they are family or spouses. If someone enters the room after all are seated, and it means this new person will have to sit next to the opposite sex, others will get up and move around so it works out right again. If they enter and find there is only one empty seat and the wrong gender is on the other half of it, they just pause and look around the room, and someone will get up and move. I recently read an article suggesting that this custom had died out and now was only happening in villages. However, it still happens at dinner parties in upper class, Westernised, Muslim, Beiruti social circles. The difference may be that very close family friends will sit next to each other. The same happens in car travel. I will often give my front seat so that an unrelated man and woman don't have to sit together in the back seat. The male passenger goes in front with the male driver. Riding in shared taxis (called "serveece") is the same. Women will refuse to ride in a taxi filled with men if there is only one place left. They wait for the next appropriate one. Women do not take the front seat with the driver if alone, but may decide to move up front if other men get in the back along the route. If men and women share a taxi, they keep some distance between them. I rode in a taxi with a young Christian woman in Amman, Jordan. When it stopped for us, there was a young man already seated in the far side. We both got in the back with him, but she glared at him and shoved her handbag between them in a very dramatic manner. The offending male crouched in his corner until he could escape at his stop.

Christian and Muslim segregation?

In many countries there is typically minimised social contact between the Muslim majority and the Christian minority. Can the minority local Christians teach us how to live in local Muslim culture? It depends whether they share the same culture. The answer will vary according to who you ask. Local Christians responded from one end of the spectrum to the other: from "There is no difference between us and we share a common Arab (or Eastern) culture" to "We have nothing in common at all." So I will have to fill the gap with my experiences of living in countries where there is a Christian minority: Egypt, Jordan, Syria and Lebanon. Both responses are true.

When I lived with an Arab Christian family in Amman, the elderly grandmother frequently took me out onto the balcony and told me about the awful "dirty" Muslims who lived in the nearby houses. I observed her house and theirs, and saw no difference at all. I had a similar experience in Sydney in the 1970s. A Middle Eastern Christian pointed out Turkish neighbours, telling me that Turks are dirty people and that they "eat on the floor". By this she meant they are of low status, but I did not understand this. I had never known a Turk and wasn't sure where Turkey was, nor had I ever seen people eat *off* the floor, so it sounded terrible and it backed up her point. I pictured people sitting on the bare floor, eating off their plates in front of them. Years later, I visited Turkey and found that the people are fastidious about cleanliness in their homes. (Public spaces are a different matter and remind us to learn how other cultures view use of public space. They may not consider themselves responsible for it.) Turks clean and shine the marble steps to their house, and dump garbage around the corner. They will not allow shoes in the house, in order to keep street dirt out and floors clean. If they eat on the floor, it is treated as a dining table and spread with special mats and a cloth. I think my friend had imbibed attitudes from past Christian Arab generations under Muslim Turkish imperialism.

Another Middle Eastern Christian impressed upon me that even the ways Muslim and Christian families relate to each other is totally different, because the Christians are kind and honourable and have table manners.

These types of comments, from both Muslims and Christians, backed up the general impression I gained that Muslims and Christians of the same nationality can live in two different worlds, sometimes with different cultural practices. The Christians struggle with being treated as second-class citizens and can live in reaction to the predominant culture. In some Muslim countries today, Christians are still enduring fierce persecution. There can be great hostility between the two groups. Christians from various Arab countries have told me, "I am not Arab. I am [Egyptian or Lebanese or Jordanian etc.]." The problem is that these Christians are falling into a typical Muslim misconception: Arab equals Muslim. It didn't before Islam, and it still doesn't, and I would encourage Christian Arabs to preserve their claims to an Arab identity. The Arabic language spread with the Arab conquests through the Middle East and north Africa, and Arab became identified with Islam. It has also become a political term, as numbers of people who formerly did not call themselves Arab now use this term. This is why some local Christians do not want the Arab label. Some Christians give their children Western names, avoiding Arab names because Muslims also have these names. Hence when you meet an Arab with a Western name you can be pretty sure that person is a Christian. These different names are cues when people meet. They know the other person's religion immediately and often this will mean that they will not befriend the person.

One of our Egyptian friends was a pastor in Egypt. He arrived at our house and joined the other four men sitting in the living room. When he realised that he was the only Christian, he became unusually quiet and tense. Eventually he loosened up and enjoyed the company. Later, he told us that this was the first time he had been in such close social contact with Muslims. He had not gone out of his way to avoid them; he had just not been in the same social circles. On another occasion, we arranged to take a group of American tourists to talk with a sheikh about Islam. They were studying comparative religion and had been studying the rudiments of Islam. We met at Al Azhar, one of the world's most famous university centres and Muslim missionary training mosques. Tourists come from all over the globe to visit this beautiful and historical place of worship. After introductions we entered the mosque. The Americans all stopped at the door to remove their shoes, and women covered their heads. Suddenly, we heard a commotion. The Egyptian Christian had walked straight into the mosque in his shoes. He made a running retreat, as worshippers yelled. He apparently had never been in a mosque before.

An Arab Christian couple residing in Europe visited north Africa to encourage local followers of Christ. They lodged in the home of a local leader of Muslim background. One of the men told me that the discussion centred on the insensitivity of Western Christians to local customs. But during the discussion the men were looking uncomfortable, and kept changing chairs. The Arab woman had just returned from the beach and was wearing shorts, and the men opposite her found themselves looking up her thighs. Either the couple had resided so long in Europe that they had lost sensitivity to their former culture, or they had lived in a Western way in the former country. The host was held responsible because he allowed this to happen in his home.

I have chosen my positive example from a Lebanese

Christian woman. She lived among many Muslim neighbours in a different country. One of her neighbours was very distressed because her young brother was jailed for joining in a demonstration. Getting out of jail can be very difficult. The Christian woman told her, "I feel very sad with you for your brother. I know God cares for him, so will pray that he gets freed." A couple of weeks later, the Muslim lady arrived on her doorstep full of joy. "A miracle happened. He's free!" This Arab Christian's advice to us is "God wants us to be a blessing to those around us. Muslims do have some different customs, and so do the Catholics here, and many others. But these practices have nothing wrong in them and should not keep us apart. We have the human side in common. We join in their celebrations and their sad events. Attending these things doesn't compromise our faith in any way. Look, this where Jesus loved to spend his time. And he got criticised for being with the wrong kind of people! Those who wouldn't mix with Jesus' friends called them 'sinners'. Women particularly can share in each other's lives, helping care for families. When a baby is born we can offer help, or when a child is sick, or a woman is not feeling up to the duties of the house, we can help. We can be good friends. We are called to be like Christ, whether we get a good response or not." I think with this kind of attitude this lady is not likely to get a bad response. So can we depend on Eastern Christians to teach us how to live among Muslims? It depends who you ask – so ask around.

Notes

1. Bruce Malina, *The Social World of Jesus and the Gospels*, Routledge, London, 1996, p. 51.
2. Ibrahim Muhawi and Sharif Kanaana, *Speak Bird, Speak*

Again: Palestinian Arab Folktales, University of California Press, 1989, p. 34.

3. Malina, *op. cit.*, p. 43.

4. Samuel and Amy Zwemer, *Moslem Women*, The Central Committee for the United Study of Foreign Missions, Massachussetts, 1926, p. 193.

5. Bouthania Shaaban, *Both Right and Left Handed*, Indiana University Press, 1988, p. 3.

CHAPTER SEVEN

LIVING WITH RESTRICTIONS

Western women in Muslim countries struggle with the confines on personal freedom. In many traditional families and countries, women never go out on their own, nor without their husband's permission or knowledge.

Women usually go out with their husbands, a relative or a friend. It may be rare to see women shopping on their own, or eating on their own, unless they are going to work or picking up their children from school. In a north African town, one of the first signs locals picked up that something was amiss in a cross-cultural marriage was that the Western wife was always out alone and wandering around the town at early and late hours. The family were not treating her as a bona fide wife. When the marriage stabilised after a pregnancy, she was not allowed to go out randomly like a tourist. The family took proper care of her – and both their reputations – by more circumscribing her movements.

An American-Asian woman living in Malaysia says,

This has been quite difficult for me as I am used to my independence. As I could pass as a local Muslim, I dress conservatively. I don't wear a veil even though people find it strange. It has taken me a long time to realise this. I used to do other strange things also. I went visiting my Muslim friends on my own. My friends used to say to me, "You are very brave to go out on your own!" I naively replied that I did not fear because Jesus is with me. Recently, some women who work at a shop in a shopping centre told me they assumed I was not married, until one day they saw me shopping with my husband. When I asked why, they said because I seemed so carefree walking around alone.

On another occasion a woman who was taking driving lessons with me was surprised that I was going shopping on my own. I asked her who she normally goes with, and she said with her husband or her sister or mother. She has never gone out shopping alone. On that same day, I visited some women who owned a food stall. They were surprised that my husband was not coming to pick me up. One wanted to take me to the bus stop. As I didn't want to trouble them I refused her offer (something I regretted). As I left them, one of them teased me that I was acting like a single lady and they both told me to be careful. On hindsight I should have taken their lift. They were concerned for my reputation.

Even women who do go out alone may not like to go alone after dark. This has more to do with reputation than safety. However, most Easterners, whether women or men, simply just do not like being alone. Sunbathers cluster in patches on beaches, leaving wide open spaces. People search out someone to eat with, shop with and walk with. Traditional families often sleep in the same room. Being alone is a kind of solitary confinement, and caring societies don't let it happen. It is a sign of suspected mental illness.

Because of this, it is not wise to repeat to a husband anything that the wife has told you. In marriages where women are treated badly and have no legal redress, the women often resort to cunning and subterfuge for emotional survival. The result of a wife being oppressed is a relationship in which there is no sense of being best friends or heirs together in the grace of life. Some women keep a closely guarded private life and do not share, what seems to an outsider, even the most trivial bits of information with their families. For example, if a woman is denied liberty to leave the home or visit her family or friends, she may ask for permission to go to the public baths. Women spend three or four hours at the baths, exploiting the time for visiting with friends and relaxing. Once given permission to go to the baths, she may stop off at friends' places along the way or make a quick shopping errand. If, for example, you saw her in a place where she was not supposed to be and you mentioned to someone else that you had seen her there, this trivial comment could cause a major problem and the loss of her freedom. An apparently insignificant comment could lead to a domestic row, or even a divorce. At the very least, you will have lost her trust in you.

An American woman married to an Arab had an incident in the street with young boys. She did not mention the problem to her husband, as he would feel he needed to round up the boys and confront them to save his honour, and he would blame her for not knowing how to handle herself on the street. The next day, she was walking with her husband and passed her American employer in the street. He made a joke about the incident which had no importance in his mind at all. The couple returned home to have a fight about it.

The majority of Muslims live in countries ranging from the merely undemocratic to regimes of terror where the state is your enemy and so are the police. Information is power, because information can be used against you. People distrust others and fear enemies, so information about anything is not given out freely. Children are taught not to share anything about the family life with outsiders, and not to trust policemen. Anything they tell the police could harm the family. Outsiders need to go through a long listening period because we don't know what is safe to share.

Locals are always reading between the lines, looking for non-verbal cues. Nobody wants to be the bearer of bad news, so if family members live overseas they are often not told of close family deaths. One friend found out that her brother had been killed in the Iraq–Iran war, over one year earlier, by noticing that everyone was wearing mourning in the most recent photo received. When locals advise family that a close relative has died, they usually tell them to come urgently because the person is "very ill". We have had frustrating experiences where we relied on Muslim family members to pass on information that we could not visit as planned, and discovered they didn't pass on the news because, "Only God knows the future. Why tell them bad news that may not happen?"

When can I be me?

When we try to live according to local customs it can be difficult. But I believe there is a way to transform these restrictions into spiritual gain. By voluntarily submitting to the same restrictions that our Muslim friends live under, Christians can walk in their shoes. There are few ways in which Western Christian women can truly identify with Muslim friends, or can understand their struggles, because our life is different, but we can choose to try to take on their point of view and live in their world. Identify with Muslim women in as many ways as possible and share Christ's life within those boundaries. This seems, to me, to be what living the Gospel means and leaving a model of faith that can be copied.

If secular and Muslim women can give up personal preferences and submit to Islamic customs that they do not agree with, surely Christian women can do the same for our testimony. Christ left all his glory to become one of us, in order to show us the way home to the Father. We have an opportunity to lay down self for the sake of Christ. We have an opportunity to follow in the steps of the One who laid aside everything to enable us to receive his word.

Learning to live life in new ways, like anything new, can be difficult in the beginning. At first, I found it very difficult to move between the differing roles required of Arab women. A popular joke says that an Arab wife is desired to be a chef in the kitchen, a lady in the living room, economical in finances and a courtesan in the bedroom. In the joke the man finds his wife has all of these qualities, but all in the wrong rooms! I felt like a person split into factions and didn't know which one was really me, and I struggled with loss of spontaneity.

One Western woman, who is now enjoying her life in Oman, says:

> I have begun to make adjustments in my lifestyle, especially with what I call "acting"; that is, being more insistent and effusive than I would feel comfortable doing in the West. Because it doesn't feel like "me" when I behave that way (although my friends love it and respond to it when I have convinced them by my behaviour), I call it acting. But the more I do it, the more comfortable it is for me and I am growing into this more effusive person. . . . It's rather like developing a second me, an Eastern one to be trotted out at the right time.

She is learning to develop appropriate personalities for different settings. Learning to go back and forth between them can take years. It means learning to express that part of her personality that shows kindness, friendship and sincerity in a different way than she conveyed these things at home in America. A man who lived many years in the Arab world said that even when he speaks on the phone to old Arab friends, a different personality emerges. He is more animated, extroverted and fun.

Fun may seem a word out of place in the light of all this discussion about propriety. However, when I think of Arab society, the first picture I conjure up is a party. Learn how to offer hospitality, in order to host the party. Arabs are gregarious and fun-loving, and generally hospitable and kind to strangers living among them. But Arabs tend to see Westerners as cold, so we need to show warmth in ways they recognise. A display of emotion is not something to avoid. When I was mourning my father's death, I visited a hairdresser with a local friend in Morocco. Some comment caused me to break down and cry. I was embarrassed at showing so much public emotion and was trying to get back in control when the hairdresser exclaimed, "Oh, this Westerner has feelings!"

Motherhood

The recent pattern of daily life where the woman is alone in the house with young screaming children to care for, while the man is out all day earning a wage, is not a common model of the family in world history. Missionary marriages also crack under the stress of this pattern of behaviour – quite apart from the stresses of cross-cultural living. A common factor is the unhappiness of the women. "Who am I?" and "What can I do that counts?" are painful questions for many young Christian mothers. Whether women are living overseas or at home in the West, many spend years feeling frustrated that they can't be "out ministering" because they have young children and the home to care for.

How many Christian mothers have felt unfulfilled and useless as ambassadors of Christ, because time is taken up with changing nappies (diapers) and mopping up mess? Since mothers will spend about ten years of their lives primarily consumed in family care and the rest of their lives centred on it, they need a biblical perspective. If the real way to serve Christ is only street evangelism and teaching the Bible, then Christians should get full-time help for the house and children. But, since God made motherhood and desires responsible parenthood, as well as the fulfilment of the Great Commission, God must have a plan for mothers.

In fact, the Bible outlines a general ministry for women in the church and it's a lifestyle particularly suited for those years of our lives when mothers are "tied to the house". Our mandate is to model Christ-centred lives, as a witness to non-Christians and an example for new Christians to imitate. Paul continually told the young churches, "Whatever you have learned or received or heard from me, or seen in me – put it into practice."[1] If the only way we are able to model Christian discipleship is to bring in full-time house help, how can those who are younger in faith copy us? If ministry is only hands-on evangelism and teaching, how can we do this with the demands of daily life and employment? How can we expect others to do this with their employment responsibilities and demands at home? They would rightly surmise that they can't be "real" Christians, or complete the task themselves, because they do not have the resources.

In Titus 2, Paul outlines ministry in the church and he does not say, "Teach sound doctrine", as we often mistakenly read it. Paul directs Titus to teach what is in *accordance* with sound doctrine. He then works through the different groups in the church, showing how they do this by the way they live. Sound doctrine is not an end in itself, but a means for gaining a certain type of character that results in a certain way of living. Sound doctrine should result in behaviour, in a way of life that should be taught to the new in faith, not just in word, but especially by deeds. What they see in us, hear from us and learn from being with us, they should be able to copy. This is particularly relevant for those countries where society is close to the ancient biblical model and many women are still homemakers with no outside employment.

The home and children are not in the way, keeping women from "ministry". They are the ideal vehicle for a ministry to families, and every woman in the church has the opportunity for this kind of full-time work. Family ministry is badly needed in the West with the breakdown of the family unit. So many young people have never experienced a loving family and have no models.

In Arab culture, raising children is not something you do in your own home away from the community. There are many Western full-time mothers caring for young children at home all day and struggling with depression because they lack adult conversation. Let's not transplant unhealthy Western patterns. Mothers don't need to be alone and depressed. This is one area Western Christians can really celebrate in Muslim societies. Local women don't stay home alone with their small children. They raise their children with other women's children. They spend the day with their sisters or friends, and while the children all play together, the women spend hours talking. Let's celebrate this wonderful advantage in cultures that love babies and small children. Children are the perfect bonding mechanism. If you have small children you should never be lonely. Everyone around you has small children to raise, so don't sit at home isolated and bored. Go out and sit with other mothers and have a good time.

As in many societies, there is more than one "mother and father" on hand, and others are allowed to scold any child present. The other "mothers and fathers" also give a lot of affirming love. This was one of the first things my father noticed when visiting us in Morocco. Our neighbour Abdu and his grandchild met my dad and our young son in the street. Abdu scooped our son up in his arms, kissed him, and shared the pastries he had bought for his grandson. Dad said, "He treated him just as if he was part of his own family. It's lovely to see this." This sharing of children enables single Westerners to be aunts and uncles and fulfil some of their need for family. Arab children call all unrelated adults "Uncle" and "Aunt". It is a term of respect for age, but also one that symbolises the connection of society as an extended family.

Cross-cultural stresses

A Christian witness at home or abroad will face many stresses. Satanic forces actively resist ministry and the minister. While I don't think it's helpful to focus on this, but on our strength and protection in Christ, we should be aware that we may face times of battering by evil spirits. In addition to this, for those living overseas, they face cultural stresses which on their own can be enough to crush some expatriates. Moreover, those who are not professional missionaries but are working in government, or with cultural or humanitarian aid organisations, struggle with the issue of a double identity. They juggle their responsibilities and integrity as regards their professional employment, which is probably not sympathetic to them having any spiritual ministry. They work under conditions of great insecurity, because usually the government of the host country is hostile to Christian witness. They struggle with three full-time jobs;

culture and language learning and improvement, their vocation in the country, and encouraging the growth of the local church.

Often the wife has accompanied her husband and sacrificed her career or put it on hold. She may have feelings of worthlessness. She is alone at home without the support of her family and local church. One day she was a competent woman in her home country, and the next day she can't do a simple thing like prepare a meal or talk to her neighbour. She has the full-time job of being a homemaker and a wife in a foreign country where each member of the family has special needs because of where they live – and she doesn't know how to go shopping or how to cook the local food. Maybe she needs to home-school a brood of children. She may be responsible for a lot of entertaining for her husband's job, and also be learning to manage servants for the first time. And what will she do in an emergency? Maybe there is no local adequate hospital.

So Christians need to make major adjustments in their ideas of what living in a foreign culture for Christ means. Typically, Christians arrive in foreign cultures intending to "disciple" others. It's not too long before they realise they need to learn a lot from those they came to teach. We must be guests before we can be hosts.

Eventually your responses will become automatic and not require thought about how you should handle everyday situations. Personality goes through changes, or at least nuances, as we go through life. After living with Muslims you will probably develop a lot of the best qualities of your hosts. And maybe some of the worst! An American woman said, "I almost lost a Western friend when I began to criticise her choices in the same way that my Syrian neighbours constantly criticised mine." Her local neighbours thought there was only way to do things correctly. And it wasn't her way!

After many years of living among Muslims, I still get into trouble with events, and with my mind and heart. Mazhar always has a jovial talk with the owner of a shop as we pass by. The man always responds light-heartedly with jovial back-patting. One morning we stopped to talk and Mazhar introduced me. I held out my hand to greet him. He froze and made no response. Mazhar later said I should have noted his beard. Well, of course I had, but I thought it denoted an artistic type. I should have recognised a legalistic Islamist. How did that event make me feel? I probably should not have felt insulted, but I did. There would have been polite ways to avoid a formal greeting in this setting and still show respect to a person.

With this incident still raw, I was introduced to a sheikh. I did not offer my hand, but established brief eye contact and, inclining my head, briefly placed my hand over my heart . . . this was in my own home. There were other Westerners present and I noticed he greeted them warmly, but politely, by shaking their hands. Got it wrong again! When I related this to my chic Shi'ite neighbour, she said that he had honoured me by not greeting me, so I should not be concerned.

There was no chance to get it wrong when we visited a leading Shi'ite ayatollah at his office. The men were escorted through the main entrance with a red carpet. I was taken around to the back entrance and directed to go alone up a flight of narrow concrete backstairs to a small ante-room to wait. Out of respect for the sheikh's position, I had dressed for the occasion in Muslim dress and veil. Two veiled secretaries sat at a desk and made no particular efforts to make me feel at ease. So I had to initiate talk. A knock on another door was a signal, and the door opened from the other side. One of the bearded men invited me into the reception room where the sheikh was just finishing greeting the last of the men. The room was set up so that women would enter from the other end of the receiving line and sit down. There would be no chance for mistakes. The sheikh briefly nodded in my direction, with a slight touch of his hand to his heart, and the meeting began. I didn't contribute anything to the conversation. I was very aware of being the only woman in the room. The sheikh was remote and polite in the best possible manner. He almost ignored me. This best possible manner can make me feel demeaned, but my neighbour's comment about honour causes me to look at it through my host's eyes. The motive was to respect, not to demean. My husband presented him with a copy of my book, *Waging Peace on Islam*, on my behalf. We stood together for photos, which look a lot chummier than the event. I don't mean to give a negative impression of this sheikh. I was honoured to meet him.

We will feel stress until we have made a successful adjustment. But we can choose to live in peace and not on the attack. This is a choice. There have been cases of expatriates cracking up from culture stress. One Frenchman became so enraged by his local mosque's loudspeaker that he took his gun and tried to shoot it to smithereens from his balcony. The authorities came and took him away.

Another couple living close to a mosque became obsessed with the same problem. They spent energetic prayer vigils asking God to destroy the mosque's loudspeaker. There was a simpler and more community-based solution available. They didn't need to live under such tension. That particular mosque broadcast loud haranguing sermons that annoyed the whole street, and the locals asked the sheikh to turn it down a bit. He did. Some Christians use the prayer call as a reminder to pray for the Muslims they live among and for their host country to be blessed by God.

Then there was the man who was crazed by the noise of the

cats at night. He tried to shoot them with his BB gun from the balcony in the dark. He shot the neighbour's little maid who was hiding in bushes spying on the "crazy foreigner". The authorities came and took him away also.

A Frenchwoman had a breakdown over the barking of the dogs during the night. Her husband took her away. One of the large oil companies in Egypt gave their employees special courses in cultural adaptation, in an attempt to reduce the large percentages of marriage break-ups on the field due to cultural stress. Some employees were advised to leave.

We don't need to live in Muslim countries to feel at cross purposes with Muslim neighbours. If you choose to live in friction, you will pick up all the things any neighbour anywhere does differently, and even identify sinister motives. If you choose to live in peace, you will exercise a wide compassion and treat others how you would like to be treated. You will give the benefit of the doubt for things you do not understand, and then reach out to ask about customs that you don't understand. Then you will invite neighbours to your home to share hospitality and build bridges of friendship and trust. Muslims are in difficult circumstances in Western countries, sometimes being seen as part of the "enemy", and possibly connected to terrorists. They need compassionate people who will reach out to them in the spirit of Christ's love.

Keeping our bearings

How can we keep a balance between entering the world of Muslims and maintaining our bearings in Christ? When we come to a totally different culture we must try to fit in, in order to be accepted and earn a hearing. It is not easy to give up freedoms to which we have rights in our faith and society, but I would encourage Christians to consider adapting their roles and behaving in a "respectable manner" as a sacrifice offered to Christ for the sake of Muslims.

Islam preaches that it unites all races and classes in harmonious spiritual unity, but this unity collapses when people leave the mosque. Class distinctions are more powerful than ideology. Of course, Muslims are not the only ones guilty of failing to live up to their ideals. We are all guilty. When the culture is class-rigid we will find ourselves locked into a class by our choice of residence, work and friends. So if we want middle-class people to hear about Christ, we need to live among them in an appropriate way. Some people ask, "What about Jesus? He confronted these discriminations and so does the New Testament." Being like Jesus does not mean confronting everything all at once, even if we do not agree with it. As I mentioned in an earlier chapter, Jesus always treated individuals with honour and dignity, whether poor or rich, but he did not forcibly turn the class-system institution upside down during the years of his ministry. He turned it upside down by leaving an example of redeemed relationships for his followers to implement at the opportune time.

Others ask, "What about Gandhi? He did a wonderful job of influencing people of the upper classes while he lived simply." Well, we tried it, and soon found out that we were not Gandhis. People thought we were not respectable, and wouldn't have anything to do with us. I remembered Nehru's line in the movie *Gandhi*: "Bapa, if you say you will fast until death, the whole nation will repent. But if I do it, I will simply die unnoticed."

Gandhi could influence people against class discrimination and racism because he was already *inside* his own society and was a world-renowned figure. As unknown outsiders, Christians need to adapt to the culture in order to gain a hearing. A

Lebanese man grew up in America, where he became the first Christian in his extended family. He returned to the town of his family's roots in order to witness for Christ. The main problem he faced was gaining a hearing, because everything he said was discounted as "outside influence", with no relevance to their lives.

Gandhi had a dynamic relationship with missionaries in India, and they were greatly influenced by his Christ-like life. They sat at his feet, seeking to learn what it meant to live like Christ within the Indian context, in order to communicate him more effectively to a Hindu and Muslim population. E. Stanley Jones said, "I bow to Gandhi and I kneel at the feet of Christ."[2] Missionaries asked Gandhi how they could they have a more effective witness in India. He replied that the best way was to put their religion into practice: "Don't talk about it. Live it and people will come to see the source of your power. Live more like Jesus Christ, put your emphasis on love . . . and study the non-Christian religions and cultures more sympathetically in order to find the good news that is in them, so you might have a more sympathetic approach."[3] Jones' life bore witness to the wisdom of following Gandhi's advice.

The apostle Paul outlines precedents in cultural adaptation for the sake of the Gospel message:

> Even though I am free of the demands and expectations of everyone, I have voluntarily become a servant to any and all in order to reach a wide range of people. I didn't take on their way of life. I kept my bearings in Christ – but I entered their world and tried to experience things from their point of view. I did all this because of the message. I didn't just want to talk about it. I wanted to be in on it![4]

Paul's "wide range of people" is different people-groups: Jews and Gentiles who lived with different customs. The basis of conforming to the culture is to do it for love. For love of Christ, and to share God's love for the world, we are willing to try and experience things from another point of view. I think this applies to the status factor because it's such an important local window on the world. We keep our bearings in Christ by not taking on an attitude that discriminates or denigrates people on the basis of status, yet all the while understanding its importance in the culture and manoeuvring within it.

It is possible to live in a way that gives us respect, yet without taking on a sinful attitude of superiority towards those in lower classes. This does not mean that we exclude the poor and lower classes from our homes. It does mean that it is difficult for people to reciprocate hospitality across classes. The same group of mixed class people, who meet in your home, may not feel comfortable to meet in each other's homes. On the other hand, the class rigidity may be a factor that urges some Christians to identify with the lowly, and live with them and adopt their lifestyle.

Notes

1. Philippians 4:9.
2. E. Stanley Jones, *Gandhi: Portrayal of a Friend*, Abingdon Press, Nashville, 1991, p. 8.
3. E. Stanley Jones, *The Christ of the Indian Road*, Hodder & Stoughton, London, 1925, p. 148.
4. 1 Corinthians 9:19–23 (*The Message*).

CHAPTER EIGHT

LIVING AS FAMILY

Community versus individual

Learning a language can get one into a lot of trouble. Learning the language apart from the supporting and connecting web of social structure and cultural understanding can leave one like a bull in a china shop. It will help to have a basic understanding of the main differences with regard to the place of community in Eastern and Western culture, since most Muslim cultures are Eastern.

Community is the common sharing and understanding of relationships, celebrations and rites of passage. The meanings people share are rooted in their social system. This refers to the general ways in which a society gives its members a socially meaningful way to live. It includes culture, i.e. the accepted ways of interpreting the world and everything in it; and social structures, i.e. the accepted ways of doing things, such as having babies, working, governing, worshipping and under-standing God; and the accepted way of being a person and having self-understanding. People learn these meanings along with their language in the process of growing up in their society.[1]

The Western Christian comes from the culture of the West that is focused on the personal and individualistic. It teaches that what you amass and control is more important than what sort of person you are. How much and how many defines how successful you are. Successful individuals are honoured to the point of worship. They stand out from the group, and are hallowed.[2] The successful individual is particularly honoured in US culture as he or she epitomises the frontier dream of the individual conquering the world and successfully realising the pursuit of happiness. Happiness is equated with success, which is power and money. The self-made person, who did it without anyone's help, is moved further up the ladder of esteem. "God helps those who help themselves." This latter belief still gets me into trouble at times when I should be dependent on others, but try to be independent. After an operation I was frustrated about being on crutches and unable to do things for myself. I hated asking for help. So I balanced on one crutch and tried to use the other as a hand. I discovered there is a good reason for using two crutches to balance, and for relying on others for support. I came crashing down. This dislike of dependency is typical of current Western culture.

The old order in the West, by which I mean pre-second world war, used to have an ethic of common good which said that we are interdependent and need to have respect and take responsibility for one another. This provided community plus stability and identity, but along with coercion, patriarchy and rigidly drawn social lines. But it has been replaced by the ethic of competitive individualism which believes that my duty is to do whatever is in my best interests.[3]

Our current age has the virtues of freedom, opportunity,

flexibility and choice. We now try not to discriminate on the basis of gender any longer in the allocation of jobs. However, with all these virtues are the vices of high mobility, loss of rootedness and a profound loss of meaning because our relationships to one another are seen as transient and expendable. Our privatised existence declares that freedom is found in expansion of personal choice.[4]

This is echoed in our understanding of salvation. It's usually a message of exercising our privatised choice to take all that God is giving, in order to be conquerors of the wild frontiers of the world (physical and spiritual). "Prosperity theology" openly teaches that salvation is the door to wealth and power. But Christians tend to have trouble understanding the obligations of living in the community that gathers around the Gospel, and are a long way from being "one" as Christ prayed for us.

We are also a long way from the social structure and culture of Muslims in which a person is always in relation with, and connected to, one other social unit, usually a group. Western emphasis on self-concerned individualism appears deviant and detrimental to a society where one's duty is to do what is in the best interests of the group. Muslims live in a system of community living and relationships which has more in common with Western pre-war culture and ancient Celtic Christianity. Where there is no buffer of the state to pick up the pieces from the chaos of war, depressed markets, unemployment, poor health, or financial ruin or other disasters, people know they need to look after each other.

This includes allowing other people, the group, to supply the will power to control behaviour. This understanding goes right back into biblical society. In biblical morality, practices such as gender separation show that behavioural controls exist in the

social situation, not in the individual conscience. Group
members control the situation with the full force of custom.
The individual conscience is not an internalised norm.[5] Parents
teach children how to behave by using shame. They don't
usually say, "Don't lie because it's wrong." It *is* considered
wrong, but they are more likely to emphasise that it's "shameful". This reflects the same understanding of sin that Adam dis-
plays in the story of the Fall. He hid from God because he was
ashamed and he was subsequently put out of the "home". In
Arab society the consequences of sin are shaming your father
and family, and being put out of the house. The only way you
get back into the house is when an intermediary comes and
takes you home to reconcile you with your father. The Gospel
story directly speaks to these societies and the good news is that
Christ took our blame *and* shame and is the intermediary
taking us back to the Father's house.

There is warmth and security in belonging to a family or a
sect which helps people through life and which can help combat
both personal and corporate evil. The rhythms and rituals of
community life are heart-warming and life-giving. Father Elias
Chacour, a Palestinian, described the importance of community in his introduction to this book, saying, "Our society takes
pride in being conservative, a society where the family and
social structure are still the main wellsprings for our physical
and spiritual health." The sentence is packed with implications
for followers of Christ in these societies. It is the key to why
many who try to build a new life of faith by leaving, or rejecting, both their families and societies eventually return. It is
unfortunate that they thought this rejection was called for. For
some it meant a loss of physical, mental and spiritual health
because they were cast adrift from all their moorings in life.

Arabs do not expect to live as individuals taking responsibility for their own affairs. Life is lived in the community of family and friends, and friends of friends, and they all help each other in the business of everyday life. If our car breaks down we don't simply go to any mechanic. We certainly don't look for the Yellow Pages (they don't exist in much of the Arab world). We call our friend Youssef and ask if he has a contact with a mechanic, or a friend who is a mechanic. Youssef then takes us to his mechanic, introduces us and tells him to do a good job for a reasonable price for us on the basis of his friendship.

There is always an intermediary in business and relationships. Life is tough and needs two hands on the crutches for support. Life is kept in balance when help is expected and accepted. (We will return to the importance of this balancing act in the final chapter.) Whatever you need to accomplish in everyday life it is done with the help of friends or family: marrying, beginning new stages in life in education or employment, repairing appliances, or solving strife. When a couple have a serious problem in their marriage, both families intervene and help them work it out. Even in death the body is prepared for burial by the family. There is rarely a day when we are not helping someone manage his daily affairs. When I told Mazhar I was writing this chapter, I asked him if he knew a proverb that illustrates the point. He knows a wealth of proverbs but his immediate response was "Let's go and ask Muhammad." I groaned because Muhammad lives ten miles away and I didn't want to spend two hours gaining a proverb. Then I realised his response had illustrated the point. His immediate solution to my request for help was to go to a friend to find the answer, even though I am certain he had the answer at his fingertips. We cannot live without this mutual dependence on each other.

When Mazhar is away travelling, our local friends call me every day to offer practical help. They think of the areas that may be difficult for me as a woman to deal with, and specifically offer to do these tasks for me. (Many men buy the meat and vegetables in the Arab world. There is usually a noisy crush and the need for hard bargaining, so the men protect their wives from needing to deal with this and take over this area. Some men have different motives: they don't want their wives jostled and touched by other men, or they want to control the household finances themselves, or they don't want to give their wives the opportunity to mix with other men.)

Friends will never say they cannot help. They may not come as they promised, but they will not say "No". Just as we rely on friends to help us when needed, this works the other way as well. When our friends are away, we help the family in the same ways.

Arabs do not belong to themselves; they belong to each other. Margaret Thatcher in an infamous comment, declared, "There is no community; there is only the individual."[6] If this extreme statement was describing the Arab world, it would have to be "In the Arab world there is no individual; there is only community." The Western attitude of being an individual in control of your life, and not dependent on anyone, is totally foreign and seen as deviant and dangerous to the group. So to be cut off from the mutual aid of society is the greatest disaster imaginable. The importance of this for Eastern followers of Christ cannot be stressed enough.

Westerners who live with Arab families all complain about the lack of privacy. There are no closed doors in the house. It is not possible to close the door and be alone. These literally open doors are telling us that we cannot shut out others and live our own independent lives.

It should be helpful to Westerners to realise that Muslims today live in cultures that are close to biblical culture. Western individualism is still a totally alien way of being a person in many regions. It is seen as rather peculiar in the context of world cultures.[7]

Arabs define themselves in terms of the groups they belong to. The first question asked in the Middle East is "What house do you belong to?" They don't want my address, they want my family. Where do you fit into our system of belonging? There is no slot for an individual. Usually the person will find some relationship to my house: they know a Mallouhi, they are vaguely related to one, or they know someone from our town, so now we have a connecting thread in the web and are more comfortable.

Locals define themselves by the clan they are embedded in. They think of themselves as part of this group, family, religious clan, ethnic identity, and lastly politically – as their ethnicity may not be their political identity. In the day of the nation state, many ethnic groups do not have a state. These societies think of others as embedded in their own clan too, part of the mass of Americans, or British. It is groups that are unique, not the individual person. Any group member represents the whole group.

As Western Christians, we view the Bible through our society's individualistic glasses and come up with conclusions that fit our culture. For an example, let's take how we view marriage. Most Christians assume that Christian marriage happens when two people make mutual individual decisions to be married. It is usually based on falling in love. If the family does not agree, the couple will stand against the opposition, "leaving mother and father to become one". But this is not the only biblical model. Easterners will find models for arranged marriages to total strangers, based on the benefit and honour gained for the family. In fact, if you read with these glasses, you will discover there are more biblical examples for their way than the West's. On this pattern, love happens *after* marriage.

Muslims tend to live in collectivist societies.[8] These societies believe few things need to be spelled out, as people are socialised to learn them from childhood. They share understood ways of perceiving and acting. For example, helping a person in need obligates the person helped, maybe for the rest of his or her life. There is no need to spell this out at the time. Everyone is reading from the same page. But this fact is invisible writing between the lines and is not obvious to an outsider.

European society is individualistic. Everything is spelled out, leaving little to the imagination, and life is described by the legalities, down to which colouring is allowed in edible products. When individualistic members come into collectivistic societies they do not know what is assumed between the lines. This will take a lot longer to learn than the language, and one of the reasons is that we don't know what to ask. We may not realise that we don't actually know what's going on. What we will notice is that we bump against different ways of doing things and seeing things. This story from an American teacher in the Arabian Gulf gives an example:

> A student of mine, who is quite intelligent, was caught cheating on a test in the university. He was giving the answers to the student next to him. When he was confronted with this fact, he responded to the instructor, saying, "I know my friend must study and learn for himself, but it's not our fault we were cheating. It's your fault! If you don't want us to cheat, then don't seat us next to each other. As for me, if my friend asks for help, I have no choice but to help him."

The community is stronger than the individual. In the West, we would be concerned about our personal risk of being caught, but the student saw the greater risk of being known not to help a friend. There is also the clash between the individualised conscience, the norm in the West, and the Eastern idea of expecting the correct behaviour to be enforced by the community.

Another story from the same area shared a similar happening:

I asked the neighbourhood children if they had seen my wallet. They hadn't, but said they would keep a look out. However, at that point, I felt God tell me that they had my wallet. It wasn't too long after, when the mother of the children rang and she had found her visiting young brother had taken it. She felt very bad about the whole thing and apologized. But how to respond to the boy? In this culture, the typical thing to do would be to hit him, which I think he expected, considering the amount of tears shed in our presence.

However, I couldn't do that, and so, after a few hours of looking for my credit cards buried in the sand somewhere, I asked the boy, since he had a debt to pay in taking the wallet, to help me clean my garage and entrance. He agreed, and I gave him a broom for the tasks . . . surprisingly, he worked hard and all the other children decided to come and watch. I asked if he minded, and he said he wanted them there. The girls thought the task was too easy because they did that every day. They wanted to help, but I told the girls that this was his work and so they settled for pointing out all the spots he missed. While he worked, we talked about forgiveness. Specifically, I told him that he didn't need to be afraid of me as I had forgiven him and that there were only the consequences of this work to do. He listened and continued to work. After a while he seemed to actually enjoy the work and I told him that if he ever wanted any money, he could come and help me out, and I would give him some money that he could spend freely, without shame or trouble. When all the work was complete, he happily ran off . . . paused and then returned. "Do you think I could have a quarter?" he asked. I laughed and told him, "Maybe next time, but not today."

As a follow up to this story, after I shared it with several of my local friends here, they claimed that I did not do the right thing. First of all, "It would have been better for me to hit the boy than to treat him as a servant." When I explained that this was not my goal, but instead to teach by example the consequences of our actions, my friends stated that boys are not accountable for their actions until they are sixteen or older. It was my own fault for leaving my wallet on my desk and if the boy was sixteen (or older) then I should have called the police and had him locked up. I felt that the boys in this culture are left to do whatever they want until they are young men, and then the culture demands more than they can give because they haven't had any training.

Scripture tells us to "be good friends who love deeply".[9] This can be complex across cultures when the issues are not what we perceive them to be.

Evert Huffard describes the conflicting paradigms and how this clouds faith explanations. He explains that

> evangelical theology is heavily influenced by the individualistic Western values of freedom, equality and personal love. Whereas Islamic theology has a symbiotic relationship with a community deeply rooted in the group-oriented pre-Islamic Arab culture that champions the virtues of honour, authority and loyalty.[10]

So sharing the Gospel message is more complex than one would first believe. What is the message of the Gospel in an Eastern context? What are the claims of an Eastern Christ on Eastern people living in cultures closer to ancient Palestinian culture than modern Western Christians?

The bottom-line value for relationships in family and society, and in theology, for Muslims is honour. For Westerners and Christians it is love. These most important values of each culture, love and honour, find their fullest expression in the family, which we will look at in more detail in the next section. Muslims believe God would not abandon his great prophet Jesus to a shameful death on the cross. They defend God's honour and Christ's honour by claiming God rescued him before he died. Our insistence that God let Jesus die because he loved us, does nothing to touch this argument of honour. Muslims are convinced they honour Christ more than we do. Moreover, a call to make an individual decision to follow Christ as a personal Saviour in response to his love for us is just not in their frame of reference. If it is perceived as changing camps and joining the Western Christian camp then it is naturally viewed as dangerous, and more commonly as traitorous! It breaks the cohesive bond to others in the community. This presentation of the Gospel threatens all the most sacred foundations of Muslim societies: honour, authority and loyalty. Following Christ *will* challenge our loyalties. But that is after we have understood what the Gospel is all about. We first have to hear it as good news, before we work out the implications on our particular family and culture. We need to understand the web of society, and the deeply held beliefs of people, in order to work out how to tell the story of God's news so that it sounds like just that: good news.

Family versus individual

In the centre of these concentric circles of belonging and obligation is the family. In Arab society the extended family views its members as resources, not independent agents. The family takes responsibility for the behaviour of its members, supports them materially, and can be counted on to come to members' aid when needed. The family must be able to count on its individuals to give it supreme loyalty, for only then can it be a viable unit, guaranteeing to fulfil its legal and social obligations.[11]

In a society based on personal gratification, you choose your own university, your own career, and your own spouse. In a society based on pleasing others, you allow family to choose your career and spouse. Muslim societies favour the latter. Typical university students in the West choose their own courses. In the Arab world, parents give children possible choices. This usually means they cannot be artists, musicians, anthropologists, dancers etc. It is difficult for girls to choose the performing arts or nursing. The preferred vocations are the high-status and high-salaried vocations like doctor, lawyer, and dentist. Our dentist in north Africa wanted to be a writer, but his family opposed him. He used the slack time during appointments to recite poetry and discuss literature with willing patients. One of the girls in our family was forbidden to take up nursing, because it would put her in contact with male bodies, whereas another girl was encouraged to become a doctor.

Arab families operate on authority and control using a system

of rewards and punishments based on deeply held cultural values, such as respect for tradition and old age and obedience to parental authority. Obedience to one's father, even in situations where he is unfair or cruel, is considered honourable behaviour. Conflict arises when a person abuses his authority, or when an individual wishes to go against the dictates of the family.[12]

Western families also operate on a system of reward and punishment. Parents can be punished if they discipline their children, and children are rewarded if they decide to comply with their parents' wishes. In many Western countries, in this current generation, there must be some negotiation before anything is accepted as an obligation. Children want to have good reasons for obeying their parents' wishes. If parents physically punish them, children can call a hotline for the police to intervene. Some children use this as a threat against their parents. Children may negotiate, pleasing their parents by behaving at dinner with guests *if* they are rewarded. In Western families children are often allowed, or encouraged, to be absent when their parents have guests. It is also not unusual to enter a home and not be greeted by a child or teenager.

In Arab homes, if someone arrives in the midst of a family activity, he or she is invited into the family circle. The parents do not send the children away in order to entertain the guest. Arabs love having children around, and from the earliest age children are expected to be able to relate to adults. As soon as a child can walk he or she is encouraged to go over and shake hands to welcome a guest. If they are shy and back away they are reprimanded with the tool of shame. They are always included in conversations and events, and so grow up as part of the adult world. There are not the problems of a great gap between adults and teen subculture as in the West. The entire family of three generations is usually at home to receive dinner guests. Teenage boys will usually include younger children in their street ball games. This is rare in the West. When our young son went out to the village green in England, expecting to join in a soccer game with teenagers, he soon returned very surprised and disappointed that he wasn't allowed to "spoil" their game.

In Arab families the individuals are socialised to fit in with the wishes of the family:

> They are encouraged to perceive themselves as others see them and to validate their experience in terms of the approval of others.

Standing out, doing things differently, or disobeying authority bring punishments ranging from the physical to the psychological, such as the show of displeasure, reproach, public censure, or social ostracism.[13]

Describing changes in Western culture over the past 50 years, Tim Costello explains,

In the Western pre-second world war generation women subordinated their individuality to the claims of the family. This often included coercion, stigmatising, patriarchy and violence, but along with this, came the virtues of family stability, security and a sense of community. The young carried a sense of responsibility for old people.[14]

This is no longer common in the West, but it describes typical family life in the Arab world today. The most common reason Arab parents tell us they left the West and returned to their homeland is fear of "losing" their children.

Westerners will soon notice that Muslim families are very closeknit. A Western man writes how the authority of parents is important in building relationships with his friends: "We have found that once we are accepted by the parents of our friends, we are very well respected and accepted by our friends." Mazhar and I know the parents of nearly all of our close Arab friends and we socialise with the extended families. This is not typical in our Western friendships.

Parents take financial responsibility for their children until they are established in life. They pay for their children's total education and all costs to set them up in their own home at marriage. In the Arab world the groom's family is responsible for setting up the couple, and in Indian and Malaysian society it is the bride's family. Either way, the couple begin life in their own home, provided by their parents. The young couple are then expected to care for their aging parents until death and, at the same time, save to provide in the same way for their own children. So the individual is not working for himself or herself, but for the family. For this reason Arabs often see Westerners as "selfish", because they are looking after their own interests.

I recently met some Lebanese young men who left employment "and a comfortable life" in the West to return to the homeland to care for their aging parents. Families carry these responsibilities which in the West are taken care of by government or privatised businesses. In the West there is a continuing movement away from a sense of obligation to each other.

Marriage

Western men often find Muslim societies fulfilling places to live, whereas Western women often face many difficulties. The men face the danger of succumbing to non-biblical models of marriage and family life that attempt to control and dominate women and children. The Bible speaks to these societies of the need for mutual submission. When men accept a public role as leader, they must be careful to honour their wives. When men are given public respect by their wives in ways that local people recognise, this should be reciprocated by the biblical exhortation of mutual submission. Fitting in with local ideas of respectable gender roles needs to be balanced by living in a Christian way in marriage.

In the Christian home, husband and wife are to defer to each other in seeking to fulfil each other's preferences, desires and aspirations. Neither spouse is to seek to dominate the other but each is to act as servant of the other, in humility considering the other as better than oneself. In so doing, husband and wife will help the Christian home stand against improper use of power and authority by spouses and will protect the home from wife and child abuse that sometimes tragically follows a hierarchical interpretation of the husband's "headship".

In so doing, spouses will learn to respect their competencies and their complementarity. This will prevent one spouse from becoming the perennial loser, often forced to practice ingratiating or deceitful manipulation to protect self-esteem. By establishing their marriage on a partnership basis, the couple will protect it from joining the tide of dead or broken marriages resulting from marital inequities.[15]

Western Christian men have an opportunity to demonstrate kingdom living through their relationship with their wife and children. This is part of their testimony to how God has changed their life and given them a deeper partnership in marriage.

The family of God

In the Celtic church, womanhood, manhood and the family were valued and lived out to the full. Although a calling to the single life was valued, family life was woven into the heart of the church and society.[16] This is a family model for Christians to live out in Muslim countries – and in the West. The wider family of God, the church, across the Muslim world looks very different in different places, depending on historical, political and religious factors in the country. It could be an accepted historical minority community or a tiny group of local believers meeting secretly in homes, because they have no right to religious freedom. The circumstances will determine the ways that are open to us outsiders to be of help, and we will need to listen carefully to their views and concerns.

Often Western efforts to help have had the opposite result because we implant our Western individualistic understanding of relationships and our preferred methods of learning. The typical way Western Christians encourage each other is by teaching one-to-one Bible studies. We gather around a book. This pattern has been implanted around the world with the Western Christian teaching the local. In the West there appears to be too much formal teaching in churches and too little practical side-by-side example. The current way that Western Christians approach discipleship is similar to the way they do everything else in life: study a book written by an expert. The way to live the Christian life appears to be amassing enough information to parrot back the right answers.

When Christians ask how to explain their faith to Muslims, what they usually want to know is how to explain the Trinity, or the belief that Jesus is the Son of God, and a list of theological premises. If sharing faith is only explaining what I believe is truth about God, then I am not giving very much to the non-Christian. Christ himself is the message, not the book. It is possible to give people the book and not leave them with Christ.

Living in a community-based Muslim society gave me a new perspective on what discipleship means. When Christ glorified God on earth, he poured his life into his disciples. This is how we also glorify God on earth. We pour our lives into others, and receive from them, until we both manifest the character of God. This means we will need to spend much time together, just as did Christ and his friends. Worshipping God does not need to be a religious activity where we go through a ritual, even if it is the ritual of prayer and Bible study. Alex Hay describes the important part personal example played in Jesus' training of his disciples:

The disciples were called upon to do nothing that they did not see their Teacher doing. They learned to evangelize by following Him, seeing Him do the work, sharing with Him the fatigue of the road, the heat of the day, the unceasing toil, the dangers, the hopes, and disappointments, the mocking and the triumphs. It was thus they learned to preach, to seek the lost, and to have compassion on the multitude. They watched his walk of absolute obedience to the Father's will. They saw as He continually went apart to spend long hours in prayer. They knew He never took an important step without having spent much time first with the Father. They saw His patience, His weakness and His humility. They knew the purity of His life. He taught them the spiritual values of truth, humility, patience and love and trained them to be no sluggards and to seek not ease and luxury, but to pray and work, and to sow by all waters and to wait patiently for the fruit. He gave them an example of perfect love. He had taught them that the basic first commandment was to love God with all their heart, mind and strength and to love their neighbour as they and He demonstrated to them, a life lived in perfect obedience to commandments.[17]

This is a very different approach to Christian growth from taking some hours a week to study the Bible. This highlights the problem of preferred learning styles. Most Arab children complete their entire education by rote learning. They graduate by memorising the textbook and parroting it back correctly. Somehow, students have to bridge the gap between what they learned and how to put it into practice in new situations. One Muslim who loves literature commented that a book is a symbol of punishment for many by the time they finish school. The Western Christian then gives the impression that following Christ means to memorise a large book and amass all the information about what God is like and how God works. When one has mastered all these doctrines the person graduates a Christian.

When our Lord left His disciples, or when Paul left Titus in Crete, these young evangelists did not have to begin to learn how to put into practice the theory they had been taught. So complete had been their experience already that no unfamiliar situation could arise. They knew exactly what their work would be, the conditions under which they would have to do it, and how to go about doing it. . . . In our Lord's teaching method practical experience was the basis and theory was taught from the lessons of experience.[18]

Follow Christ's example and live with your friends, joining with them in all the affairs of daily life under their conditions. People do not only need the Book in their hand with instructions how to live. They need your hand in theirs, sharing their lives along with the Book. This is the heart of the Christian message. God did not rely on a book of instructions. Christ came and lived with us. As I journey with Muslims, exploring faith, at times I am the host bringing something new and precious to them, in the hopes they will accept it; and at other times, I am the guest receiving something precious from them. We do not pretend that there are no differences between our faiths, but we do not need to denounce each other's beliefs either. We share a common desire, a common longing, to return to the Father's house.

Living a community-based life with Muslims taught me the importance of the family of Christ and family gatherings. There are many other ways that we can gather to build each other up without always sitting in a room in a formal meeting. Some of the most wonderful times of worship we have experienced were in the outdoors. The group set up tents for the weekend and had barbecues by a lake with prayer, good times and Bible studies. Other groups hired large boats for four-hour feasts on the river. Nobody wanted to miss these fun times. People who hadn't seen each other recently got off in a corner and shared their lives. They followed the same pattern for home meetings. Food and fun first, and from this shared experience, fellowship flowed, and from this, worship developed.

How many times have we sat in a church meeting and felt isolated, or unwarmed in our hearts? Sometimes the formality of a meeting prevents people from being natural, or cuts across direct communication with one another. Unless there is a particularly caring group, a person could take part in worship without experiencing direct personal contact with another.

In the New Testament the church is described as the family of God. Yet, the sense of family can be missing. It is especially difficult for people to share with others if they have nothing in common and the only shared experience is the formal meeting time. The Christian family needs shared family experiences together, just as a family does. This type of fellowship should be a regular part of our lives. It bonds our local church because it combines two of the most important aspects of community-based culture: hospitality (the meetings are centred on sharing food) and family.

We grow into becoming a family as we spend time growing closer to each other, caring for each other and supporting each other. This means our homes are open to each other during the week and we meet together for mutual support. We become the family of God before we master all the biblical facts about what the Christian community should look like. Then when we read about the necessity of meeting together and of the kinship of believers, we understand the importance of these principles because they are already part of our lives.

These activities are helpful imports for Western churches. When we lived in the USA, we attended a local church and invited ten couples for an evening of fellowship at home. After dinner they sat formally around the living room, waiting for the meeting to begin. They were surprised when we announced there was no agenda other than enjoying ourselves. We all shared a lot of funny stories and told how spouses met (which often included related Christian commitment). The next day, we received a number of phone calls thanking us for a fun night and telling us that they had learnt a lot of new things about each other. It was a family sharing time.

Family has a double bind on Muslims. They are members of their natal families and of the *umma*, the wider family, or nation of Islam. Individuals are expected to waive their rights in the interests of both, and have been trained to do so since birth. New followers of Christ from this background often have a burden of bringing shame on their families, and some can be rejected. Other followers of Christ are therefore very important to them, needing truly to be their brothers and sisters.

Notes

1. Bruce Malina, *The Social World of Jesus and the Gospels*, Routledge, London, 1996, p. 6.
2. Tim Costello, *Tips from a Travelling Soul Searcher*, Allen & Unwin, Australia, 2000, p. 115.
3. *ibid.*, p. 192.
4. *ibid.*, p. 194.
5. Malina, *op. cit.*, p. 42.
6. Eric Hobsbawm, *Age of Extremes: The Short Twentieth Century,* Abacus, London, 1994, p. 337.
7. Clifford Geertz, "'From the native's point of view': on the nature of anthropological understanding", *Meaning in Anthropology*, ed. K. Basso and H. Selby, University of New Mexico Press, 1976, p. 225.
8. Murtaza Alidina, "The philosophy of Islam: a just social

system", Chapter 18, online at al-islam.org/philosophyo fislam/18.htm

9. Romans 12:10 (*The Message*).

10. Dudley Woodberry (ed.) *Muslims and Christians on the Emmaus Road*, MARC CA, 1989, p. 166.

11. Ibrahim Muhawi and Sharif Kanaana, *Speak Bird, Speak Again: Palestinian Arab Folktales*, University of California Press, 1989, p. 30.

12. Muhawi and Kanaana, *op. cit.*, p. 50.

13. Muhawi and Kanaana, *op. cit.*, p. 31.

14. Tim Costello, *Tips from a Travelling Soul Searcher*, Allen & Unwin, Australia, 2000, p. 195.

15. "Men, Women and Biblical Equality". Lkd. CBE on the Web at "Biblical Equality" 1989, http://www.cbeinternational. org/new/about/biblical_equality.html (12 February 2004)

16. Ray Simpson, *Exploring Celtic Spirituality: Historic Roots for our Future*, Hodder & Stoughton, London, 1995, p. 8.

17. Alex Rattray Hay, *The New Testament Order for Church and Missionary*, New Testament Missionary Union, North Carolina, 1964, p. 41.

18. Hay, *op. cit.*, p. 43.

CHAPTER NINE

LIVING WITH HOSPITALITY

For Muslims to feel comfortable with our spirituality they need to feel comfortable with our hospitality. This is more comprehensive than plates of food. Hospitality is not only a custom in our home, but a key into the kingdom of God. The Gospel is the story of God's hospitality in Christ. In both the Old Testament and New Testament it is a matter of honour. In the early church every aspect of church life was meant to be offering hospitality.[1]

Hospitality is not just serving food; it is a lifestyle. It means offering each person we meet a generous heart.[2] The Gospel accounts tell the story of how Christ offered God's hospitality to a group of Eastern people who understood their spirituality as being rooted in God's law and expressed in traditional custom. They had a deep understanding that there are correct ways of doing the stuff of daily life in a way that honours God. The community Jesus lived among did not divide life into secular and religious; neither do Muslims. Jesus became one of us in order for us to understand God's gift to the world, and so left a model for us. Scripture asks us to have the same humility to do things "their" way that Christ had to do things "our" way. This should be easier to appreciate in our postmodern society than it was for past generations.

It is about making people feel like they are in their own home when they receive our hospitality. The Arabic proverb repeatedly affirmed to a guest is "Our house is your house" (*baitna baitkum*). This proverb reminds me that I am not just inviting Muslims into my house, but inviting them to enjoy the blessings of my *home* in Christ in the Father's house. True hospitality is reciprocal. If I am the host, I must also become a guest. This means I am willing to graciously receive from Muslims: being thankful for their prayers on my behalf and learning from their walk with God. Muslims have given me beautiful insights into biblical passages, because the Bible is an Eastern book close to their culture.

The traditional Arab greeting for a guest entering the home is "Welcome to the guest of God" and "The Prophet has visited us." How we receive guests is very important. An Arabic proverb places importance on honouring the guest: "Greet us and don't feed us" (*laqiina wa la ta'meena*). The meaning is that the warmth with which you receive guests is even more important than what you feed them. Traditionally, a stranger could arrive at your door and expect three days' hospitality before being asked any questions. My in-laws had a *menzul*, a guest house, for this purpose. Among the Bedouin, whoever sees the stranger coming from afar and exclaims, "There comes my guest!" has the right to claim him. The host will then prepare a generous meal for the guest, even if it means that his family will go without. We see this in the Old Testament when Abraham hurried to greet the three angels and entertain them at his door. Gideon prepared a kid and bread for the Angel of the Lord at Orphah. When the angels visited Lot in Sodom he prepared a feast for them. Then, according to the code of the sacred duty to guests, he was obliged to protect their lives at the expense of his own daughters. A Muslim explained this story to me in these terms: Lot was caught between the highest values of his culture, personal honour (in his daughters), and hospitality. He put others before himself and chose the sacred duty of hospitality.

Hospitality is one of the basic practices and sacred duties of Islam.

The holy Prophet said, "When a person is invited and he does not accept (or reply), he disobeys Allah and His Messenger" (A.D. 26:1). Entertainment of guests is also emphasized (A.D. 26:5). It is stated that when [Muhammad] came to Madina, he sacrificed a camel or cow (to feast his friends), from which it is concluded that when a person comes home from a journey, he should entertain his friends at meals. Inviting the followers of other religions, and accepting their invitation, is expressly spoken of in the Holy Quran: "And the food of those who have been given the Book is lawful for you, and your food is lawful for them" (5.5). Hadith recommends social functions in which people should eat together: "Gather together at your meals and you will be blessed therein" (A.D. 26:14).[3]

Hosts and guests

Hospitality and an open home are crucial for anyone who wants to demonstrate Christ's love to Muslims. There are certain understood formalities for receiving callers. For example, while talking to friends of the same sex, or to couples, we must not keep them standing at the door or gate. This shows a lack of warmth in our feelings for them. We want to get rid of them quickly so we leave them standing outside. When these friends call in for a visit, we must insist on taking them inside the house and attempt to seat them. If they are truly just passing with a quick message they will insist repeatedly that they cannot come in, and we can accept their decision. But do not take their first refusals as true indications of the situation. It is polite to refuse anything and everything the first time it is offered. When they leave, tell them this didn't count as a visit as you couldn't enjoy each other's company enough and they must return for a proper visit. When you bid farewell to guests, you walk them to the gate, or beyond the front door, and wave them off. I have been walked to our car by a former prime minister and a current head of state. They honoured their guest in the time-honoured tradition, even though they held a much greater position of esteem than the guest. This is probably not the case in segregated societies when the hostess remains inside the house. When you are hosted in a local home, before you leave the house, set a date for their return visit to you.

In Cairo we invited a family to dinner and they didn't come. The next time we saw them, my husband made a great fuss about how much we worked to cook and prepare and how put out we were. I was aghast, thinking that he was making them feel very guilty. I tried to remedy this by telling them it wasn't such a big deal that they didn't come; meanwhile, he was kicking me under the table and talking loudly to cover my explanations. Later, I confronted him with "exaggerating". He said he was honouring them by making them feel that we had made a big effort. My explanations that it didn't matter dishonoured them by implying we didn't care about them.

When the same thing happened in America, and the American family got upset at Mazhar for making them feel guilty, I had to intervene and explain to them that he was trying to tell them their friendship mattered.

During a Bible study in his home, with Arabic-speaking

Christians, a Western minister sat in his rocking chair with one leg crossed over the other at right angles, rocking back and forth. No one remembers the study. They remember his disrespectful long leg crossed in a cavalier way, with the Bible plonked in his lap. The message he gave was an irreligious attitude to the Word. The local said, "One rocks in a chair with babies, or playing with kids. This showed disrespect to the guests and gave the idea the meeting was trivial. Reading the Scriptures requires a religious attitude."

Locals host guests in a formal way in their homes when entertaining new acquaintances. Note the body posture of important people at official meetings. The evening news on TV will show these people seated with back straight, legs together, and dignified. Women will place a cushion in their lap if a skirt rides up after sitting down, or spread a scarf over their knees. Madeleine Albright (former US Secretary of State) was continually criticised, among Arabs, for wearing short skirts at official meetings in the Arab world. Many people thought it was meant as a deliberate and arrogant insult meaning, "I don't care about your customs, as my country's policies will do what is right for us without taking you into consideration. The USA is powerful enough to do what we want to do. Go ahead and be offended."

There is usually a hierarchy for seating. We need to learn how it works and not insult guests by seating them in the ignoble chair. In traditional Arab society the best place is the seat situated deepest into the room, in the heart of the room, or as they say, the "bosom". The worst place to sit is with your back to an open door or archway. Guests will often sit tentatively beside a doorway, and to honour them, the host moves them deeper into the room. The best room for receiving visitors is the one deepest in the house, unless you have a segregated society with different rooms for men and women. Then the women's quarters are the ones deepest in the privacy of the house. Everything we are discussing hangs on honour and shame, even the architecture and the furniture.

When guests are seated properly, there is a hierarchy for serving drinks. There is a special order for which type of drinks are served first. There is a special order for serving the drinks. Westerners will need to find out who is served first. This is usually the person with the highest status. Who does the serving? It may be the duty of either the host, or the least important person on the social scale – for example, the youngest girl in the family, or the servant.

If the host eats from the communal plate before the guest, he or she is not being bad-mannered. Traditionally, the Arab host ate from the common platter before the guest, to show the food was not poisoned. When food is eaten with the hand, the left hand is not used. Left hands are used for "dirty" places and tasks.

All these questions – who wears what and when, who opens the door, who serves the tea, who swims where and when, who sits where, what furniture is placed where and why – all have to do with honour and shame. Custom may be totally opposite in Muslim cultures in towns and cities, or different countries, but people will be operating on an understanding of what is right and wrong that is probably not evident to outsiders at first. There is even a proper way to hang washing on the line which preserves the privacy of the family by not displaying underwear to neighbours or guests. Locals will probably make excuses for us when we blunder through these customs, but why not make the effort to treat people honourably in the way that feels honourable to them? These stories are not giving you the solutions. They are simply alerting you to the main issues I have chosen, from among many, to address.

The importance of food

The sharing of food is a very important part of Arab social life, and all of life's important events are accompanied by sharing food. There is an intimacy connected with food. This is why in some societies, men pour the tea for their male guests and the host's wife does not take part in serving the food or drink.

Muhawi and Kanaana, both Palestinians, describe the importance and meaning of food in their culture.

> In folk tales, as well as life, the rituals of love are always accompanied by rituals of food. Food is also important outside the confines of the extended family. Two of the most basic values of Arab culture, hospitality and generosity, are expressed through the giving or sharing of food. . . . The sharing of food form[s] an important link in the bonds that give the society its coherence and distinctive character.[4]

Arab hospitality dictates that you need to prepare about double the amount of food that is needed. You honour the guest by the amount of food, and the hosts continually urge their guests to eat more. At formal meals, guests will not eat the last portions of food on platters, since this would be an embarrassment to the hosts, indicating that they had not prepared enough food. We were invited with a local family to a Western home for dinner. Although they served more food than they would normally eat themselves, still the meal was just adequate. According to custom, we all left some food on the platters. After passing the platters around the table, the wife surmised that everyone had eaten their fill and rather than "waste food" gave it all to her husband to finish off.

A young Western wife toiled the whole afternoon making home-made noodles for guests. The end result was one medium-sized plate of food which the guests could not realise had been so time-consuming. It looked as if she had bought a package from the shop and simply boiled it up. During the dinner the husband realised the meal looked scanty and, in an attempt to apologise, further insulted the guests by saying he was sorry this was all the food there was, because his wife was very tired. They understood this to mean that their visit was a burden. It is customary during a meal to make the polite remark to the hostess, "God preserve your hands. We have made you tired today." (We recognise you worked a lot for us today.) The standard reply is "Being tired for you is rest", not "Yes, I am very tired"! The guests came to us the next day feeling very offended. Fortunately, we knew the woman had put a lot of work into the noodles and, after explanations, they realised they were mistaken.

A lavish table is a way of bestowing esteem and affection on a guest. It is probably better to serve the national stew than a foreign dish that they may not like nor appreciate how much effort went into preparing it. When a close relationship has been established with a family, sharing meals will be less formal and the amount of food served will be in more moderate proportions.

Some societies are very conservative about food and won't try anything new, especially if it's the wrong colour. I have cooked food in a number of countries where guests decided they would not like it, before they tasted it, because it was not the right colour. Main courses should be yellow in the Gulf region, for example, curries. Yet, somewhere I lived, and cannot remember where, there was a prejudice against yellow main dishes. You could not eat yellow food for a main course, because yellow should be sweet. A traditional Palestinian main dish is almost white, so it would not be considered tasty in north

Africa where white is not the right colour for a meat dish. In Australia, red jelly is a sweet. In America, the same red jello is served as a salad side-dish, which is considered weird by Australians. You just can't make it into a salad, especially if it's red! American friends in Australia served this red jelly salad with white cream cheese on top at a barbecue. It was on the main foods table, and the sweets were on a different table. The Aussies bypassed the jelly and no one tasted it. Red jelly with white topping could only be considered a sweet with whipped cream.

Eating together is entering into a covenant relationship. Traditionally, contracts were sealed with eating bread and salt together. This is referred to in Numbers 18:19 – "It is an everlasting covenant of salt before the Lord." In the Arab world today, when two families come together to agree to the betrothal of their children, the final custom is to seal the agreement in the ceremonial drinking of coffee.

The worst kind of betrayal is by someone who has eaten in the bosom of the family and then deliberately hurt you. This betrays the most sacred covenant between two people. My husband broke up a verbal street fight between two friends, and one declared with tears in his eyes, "He ate bread with me and then didn't keep his word."

We see the significance of the last days of Jesus' life, lived as an Easterner in an Eastern culture. We note the significance of his eating of meals with the disciples when he re-affirmed their sacred bond to each together. At the Last Supper, while eating bread with the Twelve, Jesus gave a piece of food to Judas, knowing that he would rise from that sacred table and betray the sacred covenant of fidelity.

This is still a special courtesy today, and many times during a meal, the host has plucked a piece of meat from the dish with his thumb and finger, and placed it in our area of the common dish to eat. Sometimes it is handed to us. Outsiders need to take note how, and if, this occurs across genders. In north Africa it was common for the host to hand morsels of food to all guests, regardless of gender. But the host would be careful not to engage a female guest's eyes while giving it to her. It is given to honour, not invite intimacy, so he is more likely to place it in front of her. In other societies it may be totally inappropriate for men and women guests to eat at the same table.

Work on practising hospitality. If you want deep relationships with people you must invite them to eat with you. This may not mean a full-course meal in all countries. In Turkey, for example, families usually get together for tea and cakes as often as for a meal. In Yemen, the women in the street gather every day for a prolonged tea-drinking party. In Lebanon, women have morning breakfasts together. Wherever the socialising occurs around food, we should get involved in it and host it ourselves. If a local consistently refuses to eat with you, it is usually a sign that something is wrong in your relationship. We have had experiences when locals refused to eat with us, because they had done something against us.

Hospitality is non-negotiable, and it is a lot of work. Traditionally, three generations of women lived in the house (grandmother, mother and daughter) and the tasks were parcelled out among them. If mother is cooking or entertaining guests, some other family member, or a maid, will be on hand to see to the children's needs. House help is very common in the Arab world, either a live-in maid, or a daily or weekly help. Many families take young village girls as house maids and raise them. I found one helpful way to manage was to invite the girls of the family coming to dinner to come over and help me cook. This way they got food they liked, and I got help and an opportunity to spend time with the girls. Neighbours are usually very willing to help too. If I call a neighbour for instructions on cooking something, she usually comes over and helps. Of course, I send over a plate of the finished product afterwards.

Being a caring guest

Westerners need to realise that we are given immediate high status when we move into Muslim societies. I typified most Westerners when I came to the Middle East; I had no clue about class and status. I was an ordinary person in Australia (where we pride ourselves on ignoring class, although it exists), but in Arab countries I was treated with high status. The fact is that the West is ruling the world, and Westerners have high status in the global class system. We don't deserve this status, because all around the world the West has abused its power and continues to do so. This is glaringly true in the Middle East.

However, non-Westerners will not automatically be granted high status and could have a very different experience of local culture. For example, Sri Lankans, Somalis, Sudanese and Ethiopians make up most of the house help workforce in Lebanon. These nationalities will be viewed through this grid, unless they are known to be embassy employees or representatives of globally recognised companies. The same is true for South-East Asians working in the Arabian Gulf countries.

Christians usually stand in opposition to any class distinctions, as a tenet of our faith to treat all with respect and dignity. Hopefully, Christians will reject such a class-ridden perspective, even if we benefit from it. Missionary culture is typically at the extreme end of the scale of anti-materialism, and most missionaries opt for simple lifestyles. It is not unusual for missionaries to refuse to take out life and medical insurance because they cannot justify the cost, or do not have adequate funds, and/or believe it is not in accordance with trust in God to meet all needs. Deliberately choosing friends among the "poor and weak", and avoiding the rich and powerful, also fits in with this thinking. This can also be a kind of class discrimination.

Christians need to beware that we do not come to the Muslim world tainted by the arrogance of the secular West: saying by attitude that we are leading the world in science and technology and are going to teach these people how to live. We cannot afford to be arrogant. Muslims look at what the West has done with its technology and they see Iraq bombed in the Gulf War and millions of children suffering from years of sanctions. The war to "liberate" Iraq was not seen by many as liberation, but as an invasion by a stronger imperial power with suspect motives; this is the view not only of Muslims, but of many Westerners. Muslims distrust the motives of the West. I think they have good reasons, based on their experience of colonial powers.

Muslims listen to our talk of defending human rights, and ask, where are these rights for Iraqis and Palestinians, or for the prisoners in Guantanamo Bay, or for the US Muslims being held under terrorist laws without charges or access to lawyers, or for asylum seekers treated like criminals in Australia? Frustration at the West's hypocrisy, and at its meddling in other countries for its own interests, is expressed daily. Muslims do not separate religion and politics. They see Western Christians as part of the Western political dominance. Westerners tend to think Islam is the problem; the terrorists responsible for the 9/11 attacks carried them out in the name of Islam, so this supposedly proves that Muslims are violent and growing too powerful politically, and spreading their religion by force. But much of the world has experienced the West's democracy at the powerless end of subversive plots and coups carried out in their countries. Efforts to separate Christ from Western politics are hopeless when Western leaders link their actions with their Christian faith. This confirms Muslim suspicions that the recent battles are a new Christian crusade against them and their lands. Western Christians then try and share the Gospel in Muslim societies and wonder why Muslims are hostile or suspicious.

Since the beginning of the history of Christian outreach to Muslims, there has been a price to pay. A number of Christians have become martyrs when politics and religion get entangled. In the six months preceding the writing of this edition, Islamic militants killed Western Christian missionaries in Yemen and Lebanon. Most of these people had spent many years in the host country, serving in clinics, and they were appreciated by the locals. As I was writing this chapter, a militant bombed a foreign missionary's house in Lebanon, killing an Arab Christian. We need to remember that few Muslims are militants. The majority of Muslims just want someone to listen to their point of view. This is one of the ways we embody our message of grace, by being friends who listen carefully.

If we enter a house where there is pain and anger, we should care enough to "hear" and "learn" their story. Maybe we cannot do anything, but we can listen and try seeing things from their point of view. Usually, this is the point of compassion. There are no shortcuts to being a learner and a friend. This calls for an attitude of humility, rather than pride, in those who profess Christ's name. Soon after I arrived in the Arab world, I realised that the older Christians had much to teach me. They also had experience of suffering for the name of Christ. They had walked in paths I had never trod, and may never be called to tread, and they had a depth in their experience of Christ which they could impart to me, if I was willing to be a learner. My own faith has been strengthened and my heart blessed as I have learnt from the example of local believers. I have also learnt much from Muslim women. I count it a privilege to have Muslim women as my closest friends. Their faith and patient endurance in trials, their kindness to a stranger, and their generous giving of themselves and their possessions, have been a lesson and model for me. As I look back over my time in the Muslim world, I see that I learned a lot more than I taught, and received a lot more than I gave. God needed to change me, more than I needed to change the world.

> [Western Christians] must be prepared to be humble. While they may have something to offer in terms of professional skills, they too have much to learn and receive. On arrival they are illiterate, unable to speak, read or write the local language. They are culturally ignorant. They must therefore be ready to kill stone dead any remnants of a know-all, have-all attitude. They must go with a concept of servanthood that says, "Thank God, I can help a little with the skill God has given me. But there is a lot I do not know and cannot do. Please teach me, please help me."[5]

This is an interesting story that illustrates Western ethnocentrism:

> A few months ago I was in an Indian church listening to a well-meaning foreign preacher. He apologized at great length for preaching, saying he felt embarrassed being in the pulpit because he had everything in his own country and the church possessed so little. But his apology came across as a profound insult. His congregation included members of some of the most prestigious academic and government organizations, and some of them had world-class achievements. It did not seem to enter the preacher's head that people in other countries as well as his own, had done things they were proud of, and that they had a valuable culture.[6]

Western Christians need to remind ourselves that our mandate is to share the good news of God's love in Christ, not engage in cultural or religious imperialism; not to deliberately try and change a culture, nor to attack another religion. There have been many mutually painful episodes between Muslims and Christians over the centuries, when each group has attempted to compel the other into accepting its beliefs. Muslims view the Crusades as recent history and it is still a wound that is rubbed when Christians make strident criticisms of Islam. We are then seen as modern crusaders. Muslim leaders recently said that they do not want the material aid which certain Christian groups were ready to give to Iraq, because leaders of those groups had denounced Islam as an evil religion. If Muslims are so offended by these Christians that they will not accept needed aid, why would they want to know anything about their faith? In this case, Muslims recognise Christian faith from a negative view: we can tell you are Christian by your hatred of our religion. This does not sound anything like Christ's teaching: Let the world know you by your love.

Notes

1. Ray Simpson, *Exploring Celtic Spirituality: Historic Roots for our Future*, Hodder & Stoughton, London, 1995, p. 67.
2. Simpson, *op. cit.*, p. 67.
3. Muhammed Ali, *The Religion of Islam*, National Publication and Printing House, Cairo, 1992, p. 736.
4. Ibrahim Muhawi and Sharif Kanaana, *Speak Bird, Speak Again: Palestinian Arab Folktales*, University of California Press, 1989, p. 39.
5. K. O'Donnell, *Helping Missionaries Grow*, William Carey Library, Pasadena, 1988, p. 34.
6. *ibid.*, p. 33.

CHAPTER TEN

LIVING IN RECIPROCITY

A consistent problem often discussed with great frustration by Arabs and Westerners is the different ideas of the bounds and claims of friendship. Westerners claim the Arabs demand too much from them. They expect many favours and much help. They make large requests at inconvenient or inappropriate times and then are offended when their request is not granted. Westerners often express that they feel used.

Arabs say that Westerners are selfish, cold-hearted and not true friends. Arab culture revolves around the reciprocal giving and receiving of favours and gifts. Friends have asked us to loan them large amounts of money without any embarrassment, expecting that we will do everything possible to meet their need. Arabs say that Westerners cannot be counted on in time of need. The Western proverb "A friend in need is a friend indeed" may actually be a negative reflection of our time-oriented culture, that our programme is more important than people. It takes a really dedicated friend to put aside his programme and come to our aid!

Since this book is addressed to Christians wanting to be

friends with Muslims, we will explore what is wrong with us in Muslim eyes. How can we testify that Christ has made us a new creation when others see us as selfish? Generosity is a virtue and a sign of a good person in both cultures. Why then do Muslims perceive Western Christians as stingy and mean with goods and time? If we want to be true friends to Muslims we must see ourselves through their eyes.

If a good friend asks for help, no matter how inconvenient the time or request, we should not refuse help. Maybe we cannot immediately go to the person, nor know how we can help, but we must affirm verbally that we are ready to help. We may help by finding someone else to solve the problem. Giving what the person asks for may not be the best solution, but we can give the person our time and concern. Some Westerners have been overwhelmed with guilt when faced daily with requests to help financially from street beggars, friends and acquaintances. One helpful way for outsiders to determine who they should feel obliged to help is to define their inner circle of adopted family: those to whom they are responsible to enter into reciprocal giving.

The river of time

Part of this problem is the different way we use time. Westerners have the clock, but Easterners have the time. A Moroccan commented on the Western way of blocking people into time slots saying, "Time is like a river. You can't divide the river into segments." Time does not belong to the individual: there is no individual! In Arab society the person in your presence takes precedence over a prior appointment. A British missionary was just about to leave the house for an appointment when another friend arrived. She explained she had to go, and the friend returned home. The next day, the friend's husband came to see the British family; he was angry because he had sent his wife to visit and they had not honoured her. When the lady explained about her prior appointment he said, "They would understand you didn't come because a guest arrived." It was true. "A guest came" is a regular acceptable excuse, whether it can be proved to be true or not.

So if a Muslim comes to visit a Western home and is told by word, or body language, that this is not a good time to visit, how does he or she interpret this? If a person calls for help or to chat and is quickly brushed off because his or her friend is busy, it is a message of rejection. If the Westerner doesn't call to check, the local feels that there is no real friendship. Locals feel we don't love them. They feel used. If we are not willing to give of ourselves and put aside our programmes for flesh-and-blood people, we do not seem to be true friends. We appear cold-hearted and mean. We need to learn to be more impulsive and less programme-oriented. We need to be friends whom people know they can count on to be there when needed.

Playing by the rules

Giving and receiving gifts is part of this reciprocal system and there are parameters that we need to be aware of, in order to play the game by the rules. It is actually a system of indebtedness. People build up "bank accounts" of debts of friendship by giving favours and objects. When someone does something for you, or gives you something, that places you in their debt. You owe them, and one day they will call on you to deliver. The web of debts goes back generations, and family members know what is still outstanding and needs to be repaid. They remember all the little incidents of who did what, or who gave what, and careful accounting is done of repayments and outstanding debt. People offer you things and help you to build up this account. The motive is not sinister. It is just the way society is interdependent. The point is that it is reciprocal. You cannot receive and not give in return. And those you give to should be reciprocating, if the relationship is healthy. Our poorest friends would always bring something, usually a plate of cookies or home produce. It was never a one-sided giving relationship.

Nidal had surgery on his hand, and two days after he returned from the hospital, his hand was swollen and painful. Muhammad, a mutual friend, noticed his hand and called his sister, who is a doctor, for advice. The doctor went out and purchased a cream and took it personally to her brother's friend. She previously had no relationship with the family but her duty of help extended to whomever her brother wished to embrace. Nidal will be alert for opportunities to pay back this kindness, as he is in debt to Muhammad.

If you excessively admire something, the owner should give it to you. Why do Arabs feel they have to give these things away? Custom dictates it and generosity has a high value in the culture. Westerners in the Arab world have been in situations where they admired something and were forced to take it home with them. We need to be careful about admiring other people's possessions. Once in a home in the desert in southern Morocco, Mazhar made an aside to me in English about the hostess's unusual couscous pot. Although she didn't understand the comment, she noticed where our eyes alighted and there was no way we could leave the house without her pot. We didn't need her pot, but we had to take it. As well as this, we didn't want to be indebted to her, because we lived hundreds of miles away and needed to find a way to return a gift to the family.

Acceptance of a gift means you are in the person's debt and under obligation to return a gift, or favour, of equal or greater value. An item can be repaid either in kind or by a favour, and favours can be repaid by gifts. But appropriate value must be weighed up in terms of the value of time, energy or money invested.

A Tunisian friend told us this story about his family. His cousin, who we will call Usama, married a German girl. Usama struggled with the whole family in order to gain possession of a valuable, centuries old, heirloom necklace. He gave it to his wife, intending it to be a sentimental link for her with the past generations of the family. Husband and wife returned to Germany. The world watched, as changing politics caused the Berlin Wall to be dismantled. As a sentimental gesture, the daughter-in-law obtained a rock from the Wall and sent it to the family. When the parcel from Germany arrived, the whole family was assembled to open it together and receive their gifts. The father found a rock. He was so shocked, angry and hurt that he had a heart attack and subsequently died. This was not an equivalent gift in kind. The rock had great sentimental value to the German wife, representing freedom, happiness and democracy, and probably value in the future. However, to the Muslim father, it represented the rocks thrown at Satan on the pilgrimage to Mecca.

A tourist bus was stranded overnight in a flood in southern Morocco. A local Berber family took the 20 foreigners into their rude rock home and shared their few blankets with them. They killed their few precious chickens in order to feed the guests and used most of their meagre supply of flour. In the morning, the tourists smiled their thanks, got on the bus and drove away, leaving the family almost destitute. This family gave, with no thought of receiving back in kind. They simply displayed the time-honoured virtues of generosity and help. But they obviously were hurt about the way their hospitality was abused or we would not have had the story related. The (wealthy Western) guests drove off into the horizon without returning anything.

When we were dealing in Berber rugs, we regularly visited the little hamlets where the women made the rugs on home looms. In the midst of a three-year drought we were sitting under a dead tree on rugs, talking with the women about the financial difficulties they were facing. The water supply had dried up and they were buying water from the nearest town. While we were chatting, one of the men returned from the town where he had failed to purchase supplies of flour. The cost of wheat had risen beyond their means. Meanwhile, the women were serving us tea and apologising that they had no cakes or even bread to share with us. There wasn't enough flour. One lady arose, wandered off, and returned with a scarf in her hand. She thrust it in my lap and told me to take it home for my children. I opened it and found about a pound of almonds from their trees. I surveyed the landscape, looking for live trees. There were none. This dear lady had no new supplies in the future, but out of her poverty, she wanted to share with me. This is typical Muslim hospitality. Before we left, we purchased some old decrepit rugs, destined for the dog kennel, and the next week, with the help of a mutual friend, arranged for bags of flour to be delivered to the village. This wasn't charity. It was reciprocal guest and host sharing.

We once helped friends by being mediators with the contact they needed to get a child into a private school. They considered this an immense favour, as their child was thus set for life, for graduation, for employment, and for caring for them in their old age! Mazhar did not want anything in return and kept refusing gifts. Eventually, the family solved the problem by giving him a piece of jewellery, saying, "Take this to your wife." It was harder for him to refuse something for me, and they needed to be let off the hook. They did not want to stay in such great debt, fearing that maybe later, we would ask for something they didn't want to do.

We were on our way to a dinner engagement with embassy friends and it was important to be on time. Along the route, we encountered local friends having car trouble and offered to help. The wife decided to have us drive her home, the opposite direction we were travelling in. Although she saw us dressed for dinner, and knew we were pressed for time, she asked to be taken via a shop to pick up school supplies for her child. We tried three shops before we found what was needed. Finally we got her home, and went off late to our appointment. This was a favour, but it didn't carry many points. She would have done the same for us. We were in her presence and she was more important than an appointment. Anyway, time doesn't matter. It is perfectly normal to inconvenience yourself for a friend and to go the second, third and fourth mile. What is expected is that these kindnesses will be paid back as given.

When we understand this, Christ's words about giving without thought of being repaid take on new meaning:

> When you give a luncheon or dinner, do not invite your friends, your brothers or relatives, or your rich neighbours; if you do, they may invite you back and so you will be repaid. But when you give a banquet, invite the poor, the crippled, the lame, the blind, and you will be blessed. Although they cannot repay you, you will be repaid at the resurrection.[1]

Western Christians who would not go into debt or purchase on credit may pride themselves by being in debt to no one. Yet these same people may be in debt to their local friends from unpaid favours and gifts.

The following story came from Malaysia, but the same custom is typical of numerous cultures. Two single young Western women had just moved into a new house. When asked how things were going after a few weeks of being there, they replied that everything was wonderful; every day their upstairs neighbours would send down plates and trays of food. "We haven't had to cook at all," they said. Their friend asked, "But what have you sent back up to them on the plates?" They looked at each other kind of perplexed and said, "Er, we just sent them back up dirty when we were done." It is really amazing that the local family kept on sending food after the girls treated them so shabbily.

When neighbours send plates of hot food, or cakes or fruit, or whatever is abundant in the house to share, they are establishing an account of debts to be paid back. They are inviting you to become a part of the web of society. The plates should be returned filled with reciprocal food blessings. It is not really about food, but about entering into a relationship of debt-favours and community-based interdependency. It works this way for every area of life. This is not just a domestic custom. Businessmen need to take particular note of this as businesses are run on this system.

The intermediary

The other factor is that it is not *what* you know, or what the law says; it is *who* you know. This is true in the West also, but it is true to a greater degree in the Arab world. The story of our being an intermediary for a school placement is a microcosm of how life works. All through these stories, I have mentioned needing an intermediary to do anything in daily life. Let's take another example: Hamed's friend, Rashid, asks him for a favour. Rashid wants to join a social club and does not have the contact, or is ineligible. If Hamed does not owe Rashid a favour, this is an opportunity to establish an account with him. So Hamed calls in some of his outstanding favours. He asks a friend to find someone with the right connections to get Rashid into the club. The opportunities for debits and credits go along the banking system until the right contact is found and the deal done. All along the line, a new set of favours to be called in is set up. This is how normal daily life works, and how businesses operate. Muslim societies are normally understood to be collectivist and not individualist because of the importance of intermediaries in daily life.

Favourites

There is a basic ingredient in many of the stories shared here. Many Arabs tend to be easily hurt, and take offence at perceived slights. This may have to do with the way many are raised, which has changed little since the time of the biblical patriarchs. Parents often have a favourite child and lavish affection and acceptance on this one at the expense of the other siblings. How often has a parent told us, "This is the one I love most." The other siblings stand watching silently, wounded. Many are the not-so-loved children with emotional scars of rejection, who do not feel important enough. I believe this is why people in Arab societies can be so upset over things that seem trivial to Westerners; they complain that we didn't honour them by enough food or effort, that their cup is not so full as another's, that we visited another more times, that we kissed another more times, etc. Jealousy is often a problem in relationships and I believe this is the root cause. The Genesis account shows the havoc this caused in families, between Jacob and Esau, between Joseph and his brothers, and it still causes emotional and spiritual havoc today. When people talk about their favourite child, or ask you which is your favourite child, take this chance to tell the biblical stories and share what God has to say about this. Tell them God has no favourites. When we go the extra mile to show someone he or she is important to us by a lavish meal, or a daily phone call, or a small gift, we minister to the heartfelt need to feel significant and worthy to be loved. Jesus always ministered loving care for the individual and showed that he knew and cared about the details of his or her life. Everyone is a favourite in God's family.

By now the reader may be getting worried that the end of the story is approaching and there is no sign of expected advice. This was supposed to be about sharing our faith and there has still not been a chart of the best ten steps to explain our faith to Muslims, nor the best 20 illustrations of the Trinity, nor the solution to the problem of Jesus as the "Son of God". And by quickly flipping to the final few pages you will not unearth them.

Muslims do not want to hear the theological beliefs of not-very-nice people. Neither would anyone. If by your non-verbal communication you told your Muslim friend that he or she is not important to you, and by your appearance and actions that you have few moral or spiritual aspirations, then there is no point in telling him or her about your faith that changed your life and made you into a new creation. This new creation may not be looking so good! We embody the message. When Muslims do not believe our creed, nor understand our message, the truest witness is our lives.

Living for Christ

We need to live in a way that looks godly to Muslims if we want them to listen to our message. When we attempt to demonstrate spiritual values in ways understood by Muslims, they should be able to see that their stereotypes of Christians, and particularly Western Christians, are faulty. Then when they share our lives in our homes, they will see different dynamics in family relationships. These examples will not be shocking or threatening to them. As in Muslim ideal family relationships, the husband and father is respected, gender-associated roles are distinct, and children respect authority and their parents respect them; but they should also see that the wife is valued for herself, not just as a mother, and that she is treated with respect by her husband and children. This mutual respect and embracing of biblical roles results in harmony in relationships. These basic components of Muslim culture: appearances, hospitality, and binding family relationships, are things we see or sense happening around us daily. But in the words of the proverb, "We can't see the forest for the trees."

Some readers will be feeling overwhelmed: "I had no idea it was so different. I don't know where or how to start, so I will forget it." Please remember that I am sharing almost 30 years of life in these few pages and I have had a Muslim family to guide me. It would have been very helpful if the practical books on cross-cultural living that are available now, were around when I needed them. They weren't, and so I made many mistakes and took a long time to learn things. If we are too afraid of making mistakes, we will never do anything.

Let's remind ourselves that what we want to do is to love Muslims for Christ's sake. There is one golden rule for how to do this: love others as you love yourself and treat them how you want to be treated. This book just fills in some of the gaps on how to do that across two very different cultures. This is not a textbook to be memorised, so that you can graduate as a friend to Muslims! You can only graduate from this course by going out and finding a Muslim and being a true friend and sharing your life. It is really just a matter of having your antennae attuned to listen to local people and learn from them. Muslims are usually very gracious hosts and very kind and helpful to strangers in their communities. They appreciate the person who makes the effort to learn their customs and language. Then you can relax and join in the party.

Christians who plan to live in Muslim societies could not follow better advice than that offered by E. Stanley Jones, the famous Methodist missionary to India and close friend of Gandhi, who established the "round table" approach and Christian ashrams for the purpose of religious dialogue around the person of Christ. Jones advises,

> I felt that we who come from a foreign land should have the inward feeling, if not the outward sign, of being adopted sons [sic] of India, and we should offer our message as homage to our adopted land; respect should characterise our every attitude, India should be home, her future our future, and we her servants for Jesus' sake.[2]

Remember the Arab proverb from a culture in which food is so important: "The warmth of how you receive us is even more important than what you feed us."

We once met a British tourist who had become a Muslim. When I asked him what attracted him to Islam, he did not mention doctrine. He said, "The godly manner of the sheikh".

Notes

1. Luke 14:12–14.
2. E. Stanley Jones, *The Christ of the Indian Road*, Hodder & Stoughton, London, 1925, p. 35.

RECOMMENDED READING AND
BIBLIOGRAPHY

Afsaruddin, Asma, *Hermeneutics and Honor: Negotiating Female Public Space in Islamic Societies*, Harvard Middle Eastern Monograph, 1999

Akbar, Ahmad S., *Postmodernism and Islam*, Routledge, London/New York, 1992

Ali, Abdullah Yussef, *The Quran: Commentary and Translation*, Dar Al Fikr, Beirut, 1987

Ali, Maulana Muhammed, *The Religion of Islam*, National Publication and Printing House, Cairo, 1992

Azadi, Sousan, *Out of Iran*, Futura Publishing, London, 1987

Barclay, William, *The Daily Study Bible: Letters to the Corinthians*, Westminster John Knox Press, 1993

Basso, K and Selby, H. (eds), *Meaning in Anthropology*, University of New Mexico Press, 1976

Beck, Lois and Keddie, Nikki, *Women in the Muslim World*, Harvard University Press, 1978

Bezirgan, Basima and Fernea, Elizabeth, *Middle Eastern Muslim Women Speak*, University of Texas Press, 1977

Bonvillian, Nancy, *Women and Men*, Prentice Hall, New Jersey, 2001

Cloninger, Susan C., *Theories of Personality* (4th edn), Pearson/Prentice Hall, New Jersey, 2004

Costello, Tim, *Tips from a Travelling Soul Searcher*, Allen & Unwin, Australia, 2000

Delany, Carol, *The Seed and the Soil: Gender and Cosmology in Turkish Village Society*, University of California Press, 1991

Eickleman, D., *The Middle East and Central Asia: An Anthropological Approach*, Prentice Hall, New Jersey, 2001

Fernea, Elizabeth, *Women and the Family in the Middle East*, University of Texas Press, 1985

Friedman, Howard S. and Schustack, Miriam W., *Personality: Classic Theories and Modern Research* (2nd edn), Allyn and Bacon, Boston, 2003

Geertz, Clifford, *Islam Observed: Religious Development in Morocco and Indonesia*, University of Chicago Press, 1968

Harland, Marion, *The Home of the Bible*, Bible House, New York, 1896

Hay, Alex Rattray, *The New Testament Order for Church and Missionary*, New Testament Missionary Union, North Carolina, 1964

Hobsbawm, Eric, *Age of Extremes: The Short Twentieth Century*, Abacus, London, 1994

Hudson Taylor and the China Inland Mission: The Growth of a Work of God, CIM, London, 1918

Hussein, Taha, *The Dreams of Scherazade*, General Egyptian Book Organisation, Cairo, 1974

Jones, E. Stanley, *The Christ of the Indian Road*, Hodder and Stoughton, London, 1925

Jones, E. Stanley, *Gandhi: Portrayal of a Friend*, Abingdon Press, Nashville, 1991

Lingenfelter, Sherwood G. and Mayers, Marvin K., *Ministering Cross-Culturally: An Incarnational Model for Personal Relationships*, Baker Book House, Michigan, 2000

Macionis, John, *Society: The Basics*, Prentice Hall, New Jersey, 1995–2001

Malina, Bruce, *The Social World of Jesus and the Gospels*, Routledge, London, 1996

Mernissi, Fatima, *Beyond the Veil*, Indiana University Press, 1987

Muhawi, Ibrahim and Kanaana, Sharif, *Speak Bird, Speak Again: Palestinian Arab Folktales*, University of California Press, 1989

O'Donnell, K., *Helping Missionaries Grow*, William Carey Library, Pasadena, 1988

Pasternak, B., Ember, C., and Ember, M., *Sex, Gender and Kinship*, Prentice Hall, New Jersey, 1997

Pritchard, J. B., *Ancient and Near Eastern Texts*, Princeton University Press, 1955

Sargent, Brettell, *Gender in Cross-Cultural Perspective*, Prentice Hall, New Jersey, 2001

Shaaban, Bouthania, *Both Right and Left Handed*, Indiana University Press, 1988

Simpson, Ray, *Exploring Celtic Spirituality: Historic Roots for our Future*, Hodder & Stoughton, London, 1995

Stewart, Frank Henderson, *Honor*, University of Chicago Press, 1994

Utas, Bo (ed.), *Women In Islamic Societies*, Curzon Press, London and Malmo, 1983

Williamson, Mabel, *Have We No Rights?* Moody Press, Chicago, 1957

Woodberry, J. Dudley (ed.), *Muslims and Christians on the Emmaus Road*, MARC. CA., 1989

Zenie-Zeigler, Wedad, *In Search of Shadows: Conversations with Egyptian Women*, Zed Books, London, 1988

Zwemer, Samuel and Amy, *Moslem Women*, The Central Committee for the United Study of Foreign Missions, Massachussetts, 1926

Journals and Web papers

"Men, Women and Biblical Equality". Lkd. CBE on the Web at "Biblical Equality" 1989, http://www.cbeinternational.org/ new/about/biblical_equality.html (12-Feb-04)

Dr Murtaza Alidina: "The Philosophy of Islam: A Just Social System", Chapter 18, www.al-islam.org/philosophyofislam/18.htm

"The Cultural Boundaries of Trust and Reciprocity in Economic Bargaining", Buchan, Johnson, Croson, http://www.bus.wisc.edu/faculty/vitae/buchan.doc

Arabic sources

Al Maa'ri, Abu Alal, *Risaalat Al Ghafraan*

Al Masri, Sana', *Khalf Alhijaab*, Sinai Publishing House, Cairo, Egypt, 1989

AlSayiditti (Kuwaiti international magazine), London, 1987

Al Quds (international daily paper), London, 16 December 1992

Ruz Al Yousef (magazine), Egypt, 28 December 1992

Barclay, William, *The Daily Study Bible: Letters to the Corinthians*, Arabic edition, Dar al Thaqaafa, Cairo